CPR for the Soul:
Daily Devotions for Nurses

CPR for the Soul:
Daily Devotions for Nurses
Mrs. Chiketa Kelly-Dale
All rights reserved

All Scriptures, unless otherwise noted, are from the King James Version of the Holy Bible marked KJV (public domain).

Scriptures are taken from the New King James Version® Copyright© 1982 by Thomas Nelson. Used by permission.

The Holy Bible, New International Version Copyright© 1973, 1978, 1984, 2011 by Biblica, Inc.® Used by permission. All rights reserved worldwide.

Scripture quotations are taken from the *Holy Bible*, New Living Translation, copyright© 1996, 2004, 2015 by Tyndale House Foundation. Used by permission of Tyndale House Publishers, Inc., Carol Stream, Illinois 60188. All rights reserved.

Published using self-publishing at: Amazon KDP

Cover Designer: RNM Marketing

Library of Congress Control Number: 2020918120
ISBN paperback: 978-1-7355549-0-7

Printed in the United States of America

Dedication

To my daddy, Louis Kelly, Sr., thank you for loving me until the end, 10.2.20

To my mom, Alice Kelly

My children: Landers, Lyndon & Luke Sheppard

God Sons: Gaylon Brigham & Denzel Winston

Siblings: Louis Jr, Dee, Kim & Eric

God Sister: Eboney Pegues

Grandchildren: Ryleigh, Jourdyn, Kingsley & Landers Jr.

My loving and super supportive husband: Grady Dale

Best Friends: Portia Blaylock & Mekeitha Knighten

Thank you all for your support. Without you there is no successful me

Acknowledgements

Mom and Dad, thanks for all you have done in my lifetime, I could not ask for a better set of parents. Landers, Lyndon, Luke thank you for your dedication to me, we have been through so much and your love, support and dedication have NEVER wavered. Denzel & Gaylon, thanks for always being a phone call away. My siblings, thanks for putting up with me all these years. Dr. Romeatrius Moss, DNP, Thank you for your vision, your constant encouragement, and your guidance. Grady Dale your constant support means the world to me, thank you for always having my back

Back Cover Photo by: Aaron Stallworth Photography

Foreword

As a child, there was a very popular portrait in my home that showed footprints in the sand. I would often sit and read the poem about the man who dreamed he walked with the Lord, not fully understanding how this message would be one that I reflect upon as an adult 30 years later. Becoming a nurse has been one of the most rewarding experiences in my life. This profession allows us to see people at their most vulnerable and lowest points in their lives. This energy is transferrable, and often we take it home. We can pull off the scrubs at the door, but the emotional and mental anguish that builds up isn't too quick to go away. Unknowingly, this burden weighs heavy on our shoulders. Those nurses who work with the sick and dying must exercise in daily devotions to keep mentally and spiritually healthy. When we do this, it builds mental muscle to reduce "burnout", an epidemic in our profession.

Most nurses are also natural born providers. We are the main caregivers, the most trusted; we take care of everyone but ourselves. The phrase, "You can't pour from an empty cup," tells us to take care of ourselves, a notion we don't listen to until it's too late. It is imperative that nurses meditate, pray, and give heavy burdens to God, accepting the things they cannot change and being resilient.

The authors of this book have over 100 years of nursing experience combined and have unbelievable testimonies. Their wisdom will help fill the "spiritual" cups of nurses using this book as a tool. These nurse authors and I are connected by a vow to inspire and empower innovative leaders who will serve and educate vulnerable communities. Through the hustle and bustle, we need words of encouragement to remind us to listen, receive, and believe. Use this book as your guide to help you get through things you might think is impossible. When we perform at our best, we can better serve our clients, families, and friends.

Remember David standing before the giant Goliath? Sometimes it takes a battle, a mountain, or a loss to remind us of God's forever loving presence. It is in the valley, our lowest point in which we can finally see Him, who has always been there for us. I personally had an experience I thought I would never overcome. It took months for me to finally remember to give it to God and Walk by Faith, to feel God's Healing Hand, to recall I am Chozen 2 Heal, reflect on my Call to Serve and to stand tall knowing that I am a Conqueror, I have Perseverance and Resiliency (CPR). I am patiently awaiting my resurrection.

Dr. Romeatrius N. Moss

Dr. Romeatrius Moss

Nurse, Mother, Wife, Child of God

Introduction

For the last 17 years, registered nurses sit at the top of the list as the most honest and ethical professions. According to the latest Gallup poll, four out of five Americans, 84% specifically, rated the honesty and ethical standards of nurses as "high" or "very high." With the exception of 2001, the year of the 9/11 tragedies, nurses have consistently ranked at the top of the list.

Nurses hold an integral role within the healthcare industry. But this role is not without is challenges. Every day, nurses are faced with low compensation, workplace violence, long work hours, short staffing and workplace hazards. How nurses deal with these challenges is very important.

As with any selfless profession, there can be major side effects, like constant stress, anxiety and compassion fatigue. If left unchecked, these side effects can lead to health problems, poor job satisfaction and burn out. In healthcare, the situations we find ourselves in can be overwhelming. It is important for the nurse to stay positive and choose to be optimistic in every way.

This book contains 365 daily devotions, written by nurses for other nurses and nursing students who have a desire to be the best representation of God (or we can say compassion) while providing selfless service to His children. This devotion is designed to help the busy nurse have a direct source of hope and encouragement created just for them. The daily devotions are brief for the busy nurse, uplifting and encouraging for the nurse who may be experiencing burnout and relevant for those who need to boost their confidence and be inspired.

In one year, the devotions will empower the reader and offer insight to help them care for their whole person; emotionally, physically, and spiritually (mind, body and soul). This devotional will brighten your day, and promote positivity as you care for your patients, their families and your coworkers.

January Health Awareness

Cervical Health

National Birth Defects Prevention

National Glaucoma Awareness

National Stalking Awareness

Thyroid Awareness

January 1

A Fresh Start

This is the day which the Lord hath made; we will rejoice and be glad in it. Psalm 118:24 KJV

Each day you awaken is another opportunity, a fresh start, but today is special; it's the beginning of a new year. With it, comes the chance to make resolutions and set new goals. You have a renewed excitement, enthusiasm, and determination in your spirit. Use these things to leave a positive impact on your patients, co-workers, and family as you encompass God's love for His people. As you care for each patient, individually and collectively, ensure you remind them of their own fresh start. Encourage them to take this opportunity to reevaluate their lives and set health goals that will be beneficial for their best health outcomes. Use your 'fresh start' to assist them in their new beginning as they strive toward a healthy year. Allow God's grace and mercy to shine through you this year and beyond. Remember, you as a nurse, are the perfect vessel and servant of the Lord for this fresh start. You encompass God's loving-kindness, compassion, and healing power. Use these gifts to escort others into the new day, new month, new year, and new 'fresh start.'

Trust the Plan

Trust in the Lord with all thine heart; and lean not unto thine own understanding. In all thy ways acknowledge Him, and He shall direct thy paths. Proverbs 3:5-6 KJV

Trust is having confidence, faith, or hope and relying on the character, ability, strength, and/or truth of someone or something. As a nurse, you must be able to trust yourself and your judgment as you make decisions that affect your patients' lives. The tendency to struggle in this area at times can be an issue; especially at the beginning of your career, after making a mistake, or following criticism from co-workers or superiors. It's at that time that you must put your trust in the Creator and His plan. Let your confidence be in Him and His desire for your success. He is the only one that can stand in the gap with you and for you. If He afforded you the opportunity to be in this noble role, rest in the truth of Him knowing your heart. He has the utmost faith in your ability to care for His people as you lean on Him to order your steps and guide your decisions. Trust Him, acknowledge Him, and He will not let you fail. Allow your heart and mind to be confident by simply trusting the plan.

January 3

Don't Worry, Be Happy

Be careful for nothing; but in everything by prayer and supplication with thanksgiving let your requests be made known unto God. Philippians 4:6 KJV

The hustle and bustle of everyday life has a way of keeping you busy; distracted. You rush through each day under stress and pressure worrying about what's ahead. You become so consumed with tomorrow that you miss out on what today has to offer and remain constantly concerned about what should have been done, could have been done but didn't get it done. Is that how life should be? God's word commands you not to worry but instead be thankful. Thankful for the reasonable portion of your mind, health, and strength that you possess. Grateful to be the vessel God is using to heal His people. As you enter today, be determined to be worry-free; to have an attitude of gratitude. Refuse to allow the distraction of what tomorrow brings to prevent you from being present for those you're caring for today. Your patients are depending on you and so is your family. Be determined to be the happy spirit that shines before every person you come in contact with. Don't let worry about tomorrow steal your joy today.

January 4

Stay Tuned and Listen

My sheep hear my voice, and I know them, and they follow me.
John 10:27 KJV

Are you listening? Are you tuned in? With each waking hour comes another task to be completed. You don't have enough time to get everything done so you become consumed with everything and get overwhelmed. You run from place to place, doing a lot of little things, yet nothing really gets finished. There is so much noise in your thoughts. Can you hear it? It's getting louder but you can't seem to understand it. Now what? At this moment, it is time to be still and listen. Listen to God's whisper as He tries to assist you. Tune-in to that station in your soul where God is the ONLY announcer that you can hear. Silence the noise of your mind and allow The Father to guide you through your day, through your interactions, in your care for your patients or clients. You know His voice so listen closely as everything you need is being provided. Can you hear His voice? As His sheep, you know His voice. Follow His instructions and you will provide optimal care for all whom you are responsible for. Stay Tuned and Listen!

January 5

Focus

But Jesus immediately said to them: Take courage! It is I. Don't be afraid. Lord, if it's you, Peter replied, tell me to come to you on the water. Come, he said. Then Peter got down out of the boat, walked on the water and came toward Jesus. But when he saw the wind, he was afraid and, beginning to sink, cried out, Lord, save me! Immediately Jesus reached out his hand and caught him. You of little faith, he said, why did you doubt?
Matthew 14:27-31 NIV

You are overburdened by your current life-stresses, personal responsibilities, and demands of your job. You can't seem to do anything right no matter how hard you try. One call light goes off, then another, and another. You feel like you're going to lose it at any moment. FOCUS!! Take a deep breath and focus. Re-center your thoughts and your actions will govern themselves accordingly. Jesus has a way of helping us get back on task. When you get overwhelmed by demanding patients, rude families, and less than optimal working conditions, take solace in knowing that God is with you. If you just focus on Him, why you chose this career in nursing and what the patient really needs, you will have a successful shift. Focus is the key! Simply focus on what God would have you do, how He would want you to respond, and how you can bless each patient. You will then find peace in the midst of your chaotic days. You were hand-picked by God for each challenge you face but you have to keep your focus!

Light It Up

I am the light of the world. He who follows Me shall not walk in darkness but have the light of life. John 8:12 NKJV

You are the light of the world so let your light shine as bright as the sun. Being a caregiver is difficult and burnout is common. You work extended hours without a break caring for strangers that often times don't appreciate you. Some display a blatant disregard for your intelligence, others are inconsiderate, and even others treat you inhumanely. Your patients are scared and angry as their current health status is not what it should be. This sometimes could lead them to lash out at anyone present, including you. Try not to look at this as a personal attack. Instead, see it as an opportunity for your God-given compassion to flow through. An opportunity to speak life and encouragement into their situation which just may soften their disposition. Take full advantage in these moments as it is an open door for you to allow God to use you to bring reassurance and comfort. Breathe deeply, smile, and do exactly what you were designed to do. Your response in these moments will set the precedence and determine how the rest of your shift will flow. You have to chance to control the outcome of these interactions. Respond positivity and with God's love. Don't you dare allow them to dampen your spirit, change your character, or dim your light. Let the care you provide be a beckon of hope. God is counting on you to be the light in their darkness so LIGHT IT UP!

January 7

Forgive and Forget

And be ye kind one to another, tenderhearted, forgiving one another, even as God for Christ's sake hath forgiven you.
Ephesians 4:32 KJV

Life has a way of spinning out of control at times. It can throw you off course with unexpected failures, losses, and circumstances that are beyond your control. Trusted friends, family, and relationships end due to betrayal and envy. This can lead to bitterness and a hardened heart. Don't let this overflow into your passion; causing you to be harsh and mistreat everyone you come in contact with, including your patients. You cannot allow those things to result in you bleeding on people who didn't cut you. So how do you move forward? How can you learn to forgive? Unforgiveness is like a cancer, it eats away at your soul. The Lord encourages us to forgive so that we can be forgiven. He asks us to avoid letting our hearts become callused and hardened. God commands us to be kind and forgiving. If we are to be more like Jesus, we must make a conscience effort to forgive AND throw those issues into the sea of forgetfulness also. Remember, forgiveness is not for others, it's for you!!

January 8

Persevere

Wait on the Lord: be of good courage, and he shall strengthen thine heart: wait, I say, on the Lord. Psalm 27:14 KJV

Challenges are present with each day. You are challenged to follow policies, procedures, rules, and regulations. You are challenged to live life in a way that is just and upstanding. You are challenged to take the high road. Challenged to be the best version of yourself. Challenged. How do you face and overcome these challenges? What or rather who helps you get through them. God is your refuge, your strength with whom ALL challenges can be faced. He IS the one and only person who will be a constant presence as you face this life. Take solace in the truth that He is with you ALWAYS. Stand on the solid rock of His foundation and be courageous. No matter what life throws your way, this affirmation should be kept at the forefront of your mind and heart. The truth lies in the affirmation of God's love for you, your patients, and this world. Tuck this in your soul and spirit as you go about your day. Knowing that God IS. He IS with you, guiding you, protecting you, and comforting you as you care for His angels, His people.

Obedience

Now if you obey me fully and keep my covenant, then out of all nations you will be my treasured possession. Exodus 19:5 NIV

As we go through life, we sometimes wander aimlessly. We try to figure out which direction to go as we make decisions that will impact every aspect of our lives. Our wants sometimes overshadow our needs. Our desires overshadow necessity. Sometimes wrong overshadows right. We pray for guidance then tend to still ignore it and be disobedient. Why ask for help then dismiss it? Why constantly follow the wrong path when the correct one is laying in front of you? Why continue to do wrong when simply doing right will do? You know which way to go but you chose to continue to travel the road that leads to suffering. Whether it is in a personal or professional sense, we know what to do. What's hindering you from doing what He said? Why be stubborn and rebellious? God calls and guides each of us toward ways that will glorify Him. These ways will also prevent us from suffering unnecessarily. Today is a perfect day to make a conscious effort to be obedient. To listen to God's whisper and obey His word. True obedience will result in the greatest rewards, but Disobedience leads to destruction and long-suffering. He gives us a choice. Choose your next move wisely and ensure that it is your best one.

Believe

Then came the Jews round about him, and said unto him, How long dost thou make us to doubt? If thou be the Christ, tell us plainly. Jesus answered them, I told you, and ye believed not: the works that I do in my Father's name, they bear witness of me.
John 10:24-25 KJV

Dreams and visions are given to us sporadically throughout our lives. Sometimes we take hold of them and push ourselves to bring them forth while other times we ignore or dismiss them as we doubt our own worthiness or abilities. We do not recognize these visions/dreams as God's answers to our unspoken, subconscious desires, or simply a revelation of His plans for our lives. It may be His guidance, but we allow doubt to prevent us from pursuing those dreams. This doubt is a very human response and it's nothing that Jesus Himself did not endure. So, what can you do to build your trust and belief? When doubt sets in, we must stand on God's word, His promises. Whether on the job or in your personal life, you must believe in yourself and trust that God's word never comes back void. He said that you shall receive ALL things that you ask for through prayer and belief. Challenge yourself today to build your belief system. Be intentional in mastering it, then watch how God brings you through life's maze and make your dreams/visions become reality. All you have to do is Believe.

January 11

Nurture Your Soul

Therefore I, a prisoner for serving the Lord, beg you to lead a life worthy of your calling, for you have been called by God. Always be humble and gentle. Be patient with each other, making allowance for each other's faults because of your love…Now these are the gifts Christ gave to the church: the apostles, the prophets, the evangelists, and the pastors and teachers. Their responsibility is to equip God's people to do his work and build up the church, the body of Christ. Ephesians 4:1-2; 11-12 NLT

Caring for others can be a tedious task if you allow it to be. You become mentally, physically, and sometimes emotionally drained. You should be reminded that this is just a part of being human and the duty of those chosen by the Creator. You carry the burdens of your patients, their family, and those burdens of your own. Take the time to reflect and reconnect with God daily so that you do not fall victim to the burdens you carry. Daily meditation, prayer, and reading of the scripture is necessary to bring nourishment to your spirit. Nurturing what is within and ensuring that your soul is feed is mandatory to unlock your untapped compassion. Being kind to yourself allows you to be caring to God's people. In order to answer the call of duty that God has placed on your life and to be a blessing to others, including your family and patients, you MUST nurture your soul.

January 12

Inspire the Masses

Sanctify them by the truth; your word is truth. John 17:17 NIV

Inspiration comes in many forms. You may be inspired by music, a quote, or a friend who is always encouraging you to reach toward your goals. Oh yes, inspiration is all around you. It is woven in life's great tapestry and easily seen by those who seek it. As Christians, we are most inspired by the word of God. How He encourages us to achieve or pursue our gifts and talents. We should strive to inspire others daily to discover their God-given gifts. Be the reason your family, your patients, and your co-workers want to achieve a better way of life. Let your presence, enthusiasm, zeal, desire for excellence, and genuine care for others be the beckon of inspiration that shines through your every interaction. Put your positive attitude, kind heart, compassion, and understanding on display and watch how you change lives. Be selfless and genuine in your every interaction. Let your actions be the inspiration for those who are watching you. As you care for your patients and family today, allow your honesty and integrity to speak for you as this type of character is an excellence reflection of God. Your constant humility draws others into your presence and illuminates God's hand on you while signifying His unconditional love that beam through you. Leading a life that glorifies the Father is just a simple way you can inspire the masses.

January 13

Be Encouraged

God is our refuge and strength, a very present help in trouble.
Psalm 46:1 KJV

Dark days come and go but you have to know that this is temporary. Trouble and trials do not last always. There are brighter days in route. You must go through some darkness in order to appreciate the light. Remember, you must go through storms for the rainbows to form. These dark days, troubles, trails, tribulations, and storms are all part of God's processing stage. How can you expect to grow if you never go through anything? Who will listen to someone who has never had any experience with hard times? Without these things, you would get complacent and think you could do everything alone, without God. So, what are you supposed to do? Turn your focus onto God and He will provide all you need. Allow His light to be your guide in your times of trouble. He is the Truth and the Light. He is our strength and refuge so be encouraged for He is always a present help indeed.

January 14

Who's Your Source

But my God shall supply all your need according to his riches in glory by Christ Jesus. Philippians 4:19 KJV

Life is full of resources. Whether it is a job, financial institution, friends, or family members. We tend to depend on these resources to help us when the need arises. But what happens when none of them are unavailable? What happens when you are forced to leave a job and you have no income? What do you do then? Are those resources willing to lend you a helping hand or finance? It's in these moments that we have to remember our true source. We have to lean and depend on the only one who is always readily available and willing to help you if you ask Him. GOD is the source of all things. He is our provider and much more. He is the person from which all things originate. Without Him, there would not be anything else. Never become so wrapped up in the resources that you ignore the source. Knowing the difference between the two can be the key to your peace. Always remember your Source.

January 15

Don't Quit

The race is not to the swift or the battle to the strong, nor does food come to the wise or wealth to the brilliant or favor to the learned; but time and chance happen to them all.
Ecclesiastes 9:11 NIV

We face many obstacles traveling life's journey. They seem to slow us down or completely block our way. We get frustrated and may even quit. Let us be reminded that these obstacles are not always meant to prevent us from reaching our destiny. They may be a warning that we are moving too fast or serve as a detour as we may be taking the wrong approach. Some obstacles may be a means of protection by the Creator. Face them head on. Go to God in prayer and submit to His will. He will guide you through life's obstacle course and help you avoid the enemy's pitfalls. You may have to slow down but you will overcome these obstacles in time. Stop rushing, take your time, learn whatever lessons that are being presented, and depend on the Lord. His word never returns void. Remember you have victory. You have the power to overcome anything with Christ. Never give up and don't ever quit.

January 16

A Grateful Heart

Give thanks in all circumstances; for this is God's will for you in Christ Jesus. 1 Thessalonians 5:18 NIV

What does today have in store? What spiritual season will it be? Whatever is in store, you must be confident and sure that you are prepared. Start each day with a grateful heart and a conversation with God. Begin with acknowledgement of who He is and gratitude for what He has done, is doing, and is about to do in your life. Talk to Him and ask for guidance, strength, and courage to face whatever comes your direction. Be confident that you will receive whatever you ask for in prayer. Rejoice and be thankful for the things He has protected you from, both the seen and unseen dangers. Be glad about your deliverance from the snares of the enemy. Allow your heart to be grateful for everything that you have and the things you don't have. Understand that gratefulness helps you refocus on God's goodness, grace, and mercy. Wrap your mind, body, and spirit in Him, develop a true grateful heart and watch the manifestation of His glory in your daily life.

January 17

What Are You Thinking?

Those who live according to the flesh have their minds set on what the flesh desires; but those who live in accordance with the Spirit have their minds set on what the Spirit desires. The mind governed by the flesh is death, but the mind governed by the Spirit is life and peace. Romans 8:5-6 NIV

Everything begins with a thought. Good, bad, ugly, or indifferent, your thoughts are the gateways to what manifests in your life. What are you thinking? Are you thinking positively or negatively? You must always be mindful of your thoughts as what you think has a way of growing and revealing itself. Are your thoughts representative of the Father or are they a misrepresentation of who He truly is? Let your thoughts be so filled with love, compassion, and kindness that when others see you, they see God's light. Focus your thoughts on the one with whom all things are created. You have the power. Who knows, you may just be the only form of God that people see. Make sure your thoughts manifest Godly actions and represent the Father today and every day.

Blessed Beyond Measure

A generous person will prosper; whoever refreshes others will be refreshed. Proverbs 11:25 NIV

Miracles and blessings surround you. Each morning your eyes open on this side of heaven is a miracle. The reasonable portion of your mind, health, and strength that you received upon awakening this morning are all blessings. Count them and focus on them more than you do on what you perceive as problems. God desires for you to prosper and grow but He also wants you to be generous with whatever He blesses you with. There are so many others who would lay down their lives to have just a piece of the miracles and blessings that God has afforded you today. Unexpected promotions, granted opportunities, and answered prayers are all simple examples of how blessed you truly are. Acknowledge all that He has provided and make a way to provide for someone else. Allow God to use you to do His will and be that same blessing and miracle for your neighbor, your family, and your patients. Remember it is a blessing to be a blessing.

January 19

Know Your Covering

For the Lord your God is he that goeth with you, to fight for you against your enemies, to save you. Deuteronomy 20:4 KJV

The attack of the enemy is real. He uses trusted friends, family, and co-workers to provoke you and spread lies in an attempt to destroy your character. These attacks can force you into making emotionally charged decisions that can interrupt your inner peace. The Lord didn't say that there would not be trouble. He didn't say that lies wouldn't be told, character attacks wouldn't happen, or you were exempt from disruptions in your peace. But He did promise that these things would not last and that He would be with you through it all. Jesus was lied on, lied to, cursed, and crucified. If we are His people, we should expect to experience and endure these same things. We are not better than Jesus therefore persecution is inevitable. You must stand on God's word and be immovable. Don't let these attacks change who God has made you to be or distract you from your purpose. There is no need for you to defend yourself and this battle is not yours to fight. He is your protector and your shield. Put on the whole Armor of God and remain unbothered because you are covered.

Perfection

I praise you because I am fearfully and wonderfully made; your works are wonderful, I know that full well. Psalm 139:14 NIV

God made you perfect just the way you are. He knew what your journey would be as well as the decisions and mistakes you would make. He knew the path you would go down long before you were conceived. The dreams and visions that you have were engrained into your DNA and was brought to fruition by God Himself. Why do you discount who you are or what you are supposed to be doing? Why do you look at your neighbor and think that's where you're supposed to be or what you're supposed to have? You are right where God wants you to be, doing what He wants you to do, working where He allowed you to work, and spending your time, energy, and effort with whom He allowed to be there. Do not get so distracted by what others are doing, by what you think you should be doing, or by your desire for more. Take care of what you have been given, be confident in who you are, and know that He is in control. You are perfectly imperfect, and God has big plans for your future. Keep the faith, trust His plan, and be steadfast.

Learn from Your Mistakes

There is therefore now no condemnation for those who are in Christ Jesus… And we know that in all things God works for the good of those who love him, who have been called according to his purpose. Romans 8:1, 28 NIV

Mistakes happen but what you do after those mistakes is what counts. Will you allow them to destroy you, dictate your future, or tarnish your character? Or will you see them for what they truly are? Mistakes are lessons from God. They are used to strengthen you, equip you, and build your character. In each mistake, ask God for guidance and courage to press forward. Ask Him to reveal the lessons and their purpose. Remember, failure is really evidence that you are trying. If you never fail or make mistakes, you will never learn anything. Do you know anyone who has ever learning anything from success alone? Each mistake is an opportunity for God to teach you something. He then uses them by converting them into messages for His people. He will take each test and turn them into testimonies. Your mistakes can be a humbling source for blessings. God is able to bring the best version of you out of failures. Just trust Him, learn through the process, and watch Him move.

Faith Renewed

That your faith should not stand in the wisdom of men, but in the power of God. 1 Corinthians 2:5 KJV

How strong is your faith? Does your faith need a renewal? No matter how grave your situation may feel, be reminded that there is nothing too hard for God. You are stronger than you may think, and God is bigger than anything that you may face today. This you have to believe with all your might. As you begin each day, you must renew your faith reservoir. You must take the time to commune with God in order to receive His blessing of faith refills. Your faith is what will carry you when you feel like you no longer have strength to stand alone. It will keep you going when you feel like giving up. Faith will take you further than anything you can imagine. It is a constant reminder on God's immeasurable power. Exercised faith leads to manifested goals, dreams, and visions. Hold on to your faith, renew it daily, and never let it waver for it will be the source of your courage on those dark days. Continue to hold on His powerful hand and allow Him to assist you through each day. Let the strength of your constantly renewed faith bring peace to your spirit as you face each day knowing that God is always by your side.

It's About God

Rejoice in the Lord always, again I will say, Rejoice.
Philippians 4:4 NIV

The chaos of life can easily get you down. Work and family responsibilities can prove to be a bit much at times. You are pulled from every angle and sometimes you may just want to scream. God knows and He understands. He knows all about your plight and stresses. He has allowed each period of unrest into your life for a reason. God uses these experiences to mold you into who He will have you to be. Don't let these experiences cause you to become discouraged or angry. Don't allow your circumstances to distract you or cause bitterness. Instead rejoice. Rejoice in the Lord always, give Him reverence and pray constantly. This is what God asks of each of us. He understands that His requests of you may not be easy and you may fall short at times, but He is available to assist you along the way. God desires your undivided attention and constant conversation. He desires for you to maintain your focus on Him. He must be sought after throughout your day and be kept at the top of your priority list. This is particularly important to Him as He prefers that you to rejoice and praise Him. He will supply all your needs. Remember, it is about God so seek Him first, do His will, and everything else will follow.

Don't Miss Your Exit

Those who listen to instruction will prosper; those who trust the Lord will be joyful. Proverbs 16:20 NLT

There are days when you feel lost, misguided, and without any direction. You find yourself traveling down the fool's highway of life as you have allowed yourself to miss the exit. You may have been going too fast, taking on too much, or simply distracted by your current life's challenges. Who knows why you have wondered passed your spiritual exit. The GPS (GOD) in your spirit provided the quickest, safest route to your destiny but you wanted to take the way YOU thought was right. You had to be in control, you had to go your own way, do things the way you saw fit because you know what to do, right? Wrong! If you had all the answers and knew which way everything should be handled, then why did you miss your exit and mess things up so badly. You are not qualified to control everything. You were not equipped with the right skills to handle everything without God's guidance. You don't have a clue which of life's exits you need to take especially if you don't play attention to God's voice. You must follow the instruction of your internal GPS and not your own understanding. If you simply listen to the GPS, you can forego much of the headaches, heartaches, pain, delays and denials. Your GPS sees things in route that you cannot so you must trust Him. Don't miss your exit by refusing to follow your GPS.

January 25

Restoration

And I will restore to you the years that the locust hath eaten, the cankerworm, and the caterpillar, and the palmerworm Joel 2:25a KJV

You have worked so hard to be a good person, dedicated employee, good friend, and good spouse. You have given so much of yourself only to have your marriage fail, lose your job, and friends walk away without warning. How are you supposed to deal with this? Will you ever heal and recover? Today is a day of restoration. Restoration of your faith, and hope. Everything that has been lost, taken, and destroyed WILL be restored and returned bigger and better than before. God restores. Your belief and trust in His word is a key factor in the manifestation of restoration. God will carry you through, lift your burdens and restore your peace. God is bigger than any loss, circumstance, or situation. Keep the faith and maintain your hope in Him, for with Him all things are possible.

January 26

Signs

Ask thee a sign of the Lord thy God; ask it either in the depth, or in the height above. Therefore the Lord himself shall give you a sign Isaiah 7: 11, 14a KJV

You have been waiting for a sign. A sign that things will be okay, things will get better, you made the right decision, you did the right thing, and everything will work out in your favor. Desperation, worry, and fear has stolen your joy and inner peace. Hang in there! Return your focus to God and mediate daily on His word. Trust the word then apply it to your life. Carry the word in your heart. Use it to be the best version of yourself today and every day. Pay close attention to every event and the people you encounter. God will provide the reassuring sign that you requested in the most subtle way through unexpected encounters. Be ready and remain focused on your requests of the Lord. Stay positive, remain alert, be attentive, be vigilant, and be present for you do not want to miss your signs.

January 27

Blessings Overflowing

Do not be anxious about anything, but in every situation, by prayer and petition, with thanksgiving, present your requests to God. And the peace of God, which transcends all understanding, will guard your hearts and your minds in Christ Jesus. Finally, brothers and sisters, whatever is true, whatever is noble, whatever is right, whatever is pure, whatever is lovely, whatever is admirable--if anything is excellent or praiseworthy--think about such things. – Philippians 4: 4:-8 NIV

Your eyes are open, your vision is clear, you hear the sweet sounds of birds chirping, the sweet aroma of food tease your nose, words flow gracefully from your mouth, your limbs move and carry you step by step but yet you complain. You have a roof over your head, transportation, clothes on your back and shoes on your feet but you are not satisfied. You have employment, money in the bank, and a loving family but it is not enough. Why? The Lord, our God, is not pleased with your complaining. He does not approve of this ungrateful spirit. Today is the day that the complaining stops. Look around at the blessings God has given you. Focus on all that you have despite of any perceived lack. Every breath you take is a blessing. Every smile that you share is a blessing. Every prayer that you pray, especially for others, brings blessings. Your mere presence with your family, friends, and patients bring about blessings. Do not block them today with complaints. Allow your heart to be filled with gratefulness from hence forth and manifest a closer relationship with God. No more complaints as your blessings are truly overflowing.

20/20 Vision

Where there is no vision, the people perish: but he that keepeth the law, happy is he. Proverbs 29:18 KJV

Is what you see the dictator of what you believe? Does what you deem as tangible measure the depth of your sight? Let not what you can see with your physical eyes be the reason you are blind to your spiritual blessings. Your physical eyesight fails miserably in comparison to your spiritual sight as it lacks the capability to see anything beyond the surface. It plays tricks on you and causes you to have a very shallow view of your circumstances while planting deceitful, misguided thoughts in your mind. In contrast, your spiritual eyes provide a more in-depth and accurate look at things beyond what you perceive as normal. When you look at things spiritually, your vision becomes clearer as you recognize that your circumstances are under the control of the Father and not man. You realize from this view, that God operates behind the scenes and He is working things out for your good. The vision you gain from looking through spiritual eyes show you the truth and not worldly lies or deceptive situations that cause you to be unnecessarily burdened. You may not always be able to completely understand but embrace the fact the God is ever present, and He will provide you with the 20/20 vision you need for your peace and happiness. He will not let you perish if you simply look at the world through His eyes. Your faith and belief move you toward God's vision for your life. You will never be able to truly see until you evoke this power. God always makes provisions for your vision so live by faith and not by sight.

January 29

Is Your Armor On?

Put on the whole armor of God, that you may be able to stand against the wiles of the devil. Ephesians 6:11 NKJV

The battlefield of this world can be a scary place. Sometimes the outlook seems bleak and dark shadows engulf you. It is at this time that you must put on the whole armor of God to protect you from the snares of darkness. You are at war! It is not just a physical war but a war for your mind, body, soul, and spirit. What can you do to survive? You have to be faithful and hold on to God's word. Hold onto His unchanging hand and allow Him to be the captain of your spiritual army. This battle will not be won by might but by prayer and supplication. Stand on truth, righteousness, peace, faith, and salvation. A war of this magnitude is fought by the Lord so do not let your heart be dismayed or your mind be troubled. Your battle is already won. God is always on your side, by your side, and will never leave your side. He is still in control, on the throne, and you are already victorious. God will not let you perish.

Dealing and Healing

'Behold, I will bring it health and healing; I will heal them and reveal to them the abundance of peace and truth. Jeremiah 33:6 NKJV

Dealing with loss can be devastating. Loss of a patient, loved one, or job all seem to take a toll on you and cause excess worry. How will you respond? Will you allow it to make you bitter or better? Will you allow yourself to fall into the devil's deceptive depression or will you grab onto the helm of His garment? The choice is yours. When loss invades your life, take solace in knowing that God is in the midst. Allow Him to be your comforter and strength. Allow Him to guide you through because He cares for you. His love is everlasting. Do not try to cope with it alone as His word reassures you that He will never leave you nor forsake you. He will provide all the strength, courage, and comfort that you need to carry you through trying times. Let Him show you His grace for it is sufficient. Focusing on Him is the beginning of your healing.

January 31

You Win

For the LORD your God is He who goes with you, to fight for you against your enemies, to save you. Deuteronomy 20:4 NKJV

Your story is fixed. The result of every decision you make, everything you set out to accomplish is that you win. You had the victory before you ever set the goal. You finished that degree, got that job, opened that business, married the right person, and your family was blessed long before you were conceived. With full awareness, you can now walk in it with full confidence while trusting God's promises. Walk, talk, and live like you are Victorious. If you walk by faith, speak positive over your life, and focus on God, He will provide. He will bring you out of what your situation or circumstance may be. He will fulfill your every need and desire. Go ahead and give Him the glory. You will live in His fullness, covered by His grace and abundant mercy. You have already WON!

February Health Awareness

AMD/Low Vision Awareness

American Heart Month

National Children's Dental Health

Teen Dating Violence Awareness

African Heritage and Health Week (First Week in February)

National "Wear Red" Day for Women's Heart Health Day (February 7)

National Donor Day (February 14)

February 1

Love Them Like Jesus

A new commandment I give unto you, That ye love one another; as I have loved you, that ye also love one another. John 13:34 KJV

Loving people is never an easy task, especially when they are not cooperative and helpful. It is usually frustrating, and you might want to quit loving them. Whenever you see yourself in such a situation, all you have to do is remember the words of Jesus. We should love others like He loved us.

Jesus came and died for our sins. The Bible said that even though we were enemies with God, He still loved us and sent Jesus Christ to die for us. In the same manner, Christ expects and commands us to love others - not as we want, but as He loved us.

As a health worker, you might get discouraged along the way with the work and the pay, but always remember that as Christ didn't give up on loving you, you, too, should not give up on loving the patients and the work. Always have your hope and faith in Christ, seek His strength, and He will give you the power to love others as He loved you.

February 2

You Don't Have to Give Up

Finally, my brethren, be strong in the Lord, and in the power of his might. Ephesians 6:10 KJV

Have you ever gotten to a place where you just wanted to give up? Well, everyone has been there. You must have read in the Bible about Elijah the prophet, who wanted to give up (1 Kings 19). He even told God to kill him because he was tired of living. Well, God didn't kill him; rather, He sent an angel who gave him food and was able to renew his strength. This same Elijah that wanted to die later lived the life that God wanted to live.

The word of God encourages us not to give up, but rather we should be strong in the Lord. People who are strong in the Lord are those who believe the promises of God and depend on His unfailing power. They reassure themselves of God's ever-abiding presence, and they keep on moving forward.

Difficult moments are usually the stepping stone to one's breakthrough. You might want to give up due to the workload you have been carrying, but remember that there is someone who can help you carry that load. Don't give up. Depend on the power of God, and He will surely see you through.

February 3

God Is with You

Fear thou not; for I am with thee: be not dismayed; for I am thy God: I will strengthen thee; yea, I will help thee; yea, I will uphold thee with the right hand of my righteousness. Isaiah 41:10 KJV

We often come to realize that we can be consumed with fear: of failure, of getting sick, of not achieving our goals and of facing a new level in life. These fears can make us lose our confidence in God. We even forget that the promises of God are yes and amen (For all the promises of God in him are yea, and in him Amen, unto the glory of God by us. 2 Corinthians 1:20 KJV).

God has assured us of His promises through His word. He said He would be with us whenever we needed Him, that He would strengthen us when we were weak, He would help us in the time of need.

Are you often giving in to fear? Or do you often feel weak and helpless? This is to assure you that God is not a man that He should lie, His words are true and will surely come to pass. Don't give in to your fears. Hold on to the promises of God, put your trust in Him, and He will help you.

February 4

His Love Never Fails

The LORD hath appeared of old unto me, saying, Yea, I have loved thee with an everlasting love: therefore, with lovingkindness have I drawn thee. Jeremiah 31:3 KJV

There was a story of a man who was about to commit suicide because he felt that no one loved him. He had a great family, a successful business and a wonderful career, but despite everything he had, he still felt unloved. This is the story of many people today.

The love of God is not like the love of man. Man's love is conditional and limited, whereas the love of God is everlasting and unlimited. People who have experienced this kind of love always have a reason to live, because they have a covenant with God, and God will always manifest His love towards them.

No matter what might have happened, or is currently happening, to you, be assured that God's everlasting love never fails. People might disappoint and discourage you, but God will always be there for you. In the same way, God wants you to demonstrate love for His people. There may be times when you might not want to love someone. But you must remember that God's love towards you does not fail; therefore, your love towards others must not fail, either.

Stand Strong During Adversity

Wherefore take unto you the whole armour of God, that ye may be able to withstand in the evil day, and having done all, to stand.
Ephesians 6:13 KJV

Everyone faces challenging and difficult times at some point in life. These challenging times are not meant to destroy you - they are meant to make you stronger. They are also meant to remind you to put your trust in God. You have to allow Gods Word to come alive in your heart so it can lead you to victory. Remain faithful during difficult times. Continue to serve and trust God, and He will honor your faithfulness.

Casting all your care upon him; for He careth for you. 1 Peter 5:7 KJV. Lighten your load by leaving it with God. Remember to humble yourself before the Lord. This builds our faith and puts us in a position to help those who face similar situations. One of the greatest evangelistic tools we have is our testimony. And they overcame him by the blood of the Lamb, and by the word of their testimony; and they loved not their lives unto the death. Revelation 12:11 KJV.

We are living in difficult times. There may not be anything that you can do about the things that are happening. You may need to endure and stand strong. Increase your prayer life, and deepen your trust in God and His goodness.

What Can Separate You from The Love of God?

Who shall separate us from the love of Christ? Shall tribulation, or distress, or persecution, or famine, or nakedness, or peril, or sword? Romans 8:35 KJV

Tough times are usually moments that test our faith. Most people don't know that their faith is being tested. Proverbs 24:10 said, If thou faint in the day of adversity, thy strength is small. Basically, this scripture is saying if you quit when things are going wrong, you are weak.

Romans 8:35 is a popular passage of the Bible that challenges us about our love for God. Jesus Christ said that persecutions are going to be part of what believers are going to experience in life, while Paul the apostle wrote that all that live godly in Christ Jesus shall suffer persecution. These things are not new, and they should not make us deny our faith.

Our love for God is going to be challenged at some points in our lives. It might be due to sickness, death of a loved one, a delay in answer to prayers or opposition and persecution at your job. Will you allow any of them to separate you from the love of God? Decide to stand and live for God always, and He will always stand and defend you.

February 7

It Is Well

Run now, I pray thee, to meet her, and say unto her, Is it well with thee? Is it well with thy husband? Is it well with the child? And she answered, It is well. 2 Kings 4:26 KJV

What would you do if everything you had seemed like it was being taken away from you?

What is going to be your confession when the patient that you've given the very best care seems to be dying right before your eyes? When your efforts to save a life seems useless, what will you say?

In today's scripture, the Shunammite woman's son was dead, but when her husband asked her what was the problem, her initial confession was it shall be well. She was very careful of the words she spoke. As she went to meet prophet Elisha, his servant asked her what was the problem, but this time, she said it is well. It was clear that her son was dead, but she refused to say it with her mouth. She knew that the same God that gave her a son at an old age could also raise him from the dead.

There is power in the tongue. Death and life are in the power of the tongue: and they that love it shall eat the fruit thereof Proverbs 18:21 KJV. Remember, you have what you say. If you believe that it is well, no matter what might be happening, it will surely be well. As you care for your patients today, remember to reassure them and speak about positive things around them. Remind yourself of the unlimited power of God, and everything will certainly turn out well.

To Them That Love God

And we know that all things work together for good to them that love God, to them who are the called according to his purpose.
Romans 8:28 KJV

Do all things really work for our good? Today, God declares that they do! David was a man whom God testified to be after His own heart. He experienced the favor and mercy of God all the days of his life, and God made an everlasting covenant with him. Many people today don't know that the secret behind the relationship between David with God was that he truly loved God. This was why he received great favor from God.

Loving God is the greatest responsibility that we have today. There is nothing that moves God more than love. This is because God is love. Loving God includes obeying all of His commandments, loving His children and believing His word. I also believe that worshipping His holy name demonstrates our love for Him. The essence of loving God is admiring and enjoying all that He is. And it is this enjoyment of God that makes all of our other responses truly glorifying to Him.

The statement it's ALL working for my good makes no sense to the person who may be suffering from some horrible disease or dealing with a rough situation. But God's Word declares on today that ALL that happens in our life is for a greater purpose that WILL eventually work on our behalf for those who LOVE God and are called according to His purpose. Remember that LOVE is so important to God. And it should be important to you.

Do You Love God More Than These?

So when they had dined, Jesus saith to Simon Peter, Simon, son of Jonas, lovest thou me more than these? He saith unto him, Yea, Lord; thou knowest that I love thee. He saith unto him, Feed my lambs. John 21:15 KJV

This lesson is about Peter's love for Jesus and the service that Peter would do for Jesus because of that love. This lesson is also about you and the work you do for Him.

Jesus was asking Peter if he truly loved Him more than what He was hearing - more than just words. Peter then replied, You know I do love You. In order to know that he truly loves Him, Jesus gave him an assignment to feed his sheep.

The test of true love is often showed in the face of need, trials and difficulties. Most times, we profess love when things are going well, but when the table turns, we withdraw our love. This conditional type of love is not of God.

In this passage, the sheep Jesus referred to were His people. Just like Peter, we, as nurses, are called to serve and feed God's people. I believe that God is talking about the natural food, but I also think He si talking about spiritual food, as well. Yes, nurses provide holistic care, which includes spiritual care. Take cues from your patients, demonstrate a Christ-like attitude and ask them how you can support them spiritually. They may need you to pray with them or simply hold their hand. God will always be there, watching you work and care for His people.

February 10

The Greatest Love

Greater love hath no man than this, that a man lay down his life for his friends. John 15:13 KJV

Most people would define love as an emotion— a feeling of affection, care, passion or desire. The Bible, however, describes love in a sacrificial way. While it may not be necessary to die for a friend, the mere thought of being there for them in their time of need is sacrificial enough. As Christians, we are to show unconditional, selfless love to others, not just our friends—just as Jesus did for us.

We are to reflect God's love and to love others in the same way that He loved us. We have to allow God's love to flow into us and through us to others so His power can be revealed!

As nurses, we lay down our lives in service to Him as we care for His people. Today, I want you to realize how crucial you are to the health and wellbeing of those you are called to serve. Keep presenting yourself as a living sacrifice, holy and acceptable unto God, in Jesus' name.

The Power of Love

Love worketh no ill to his neighbour: therefore love is the fulfilling of the law. Romans 13:10 KJV

The word love often means different things to different people. Love does not change - people do. Love involves hard work. Love forgives and, when possible, offers reconciliation. According to the Word of God, love is a lot of things. Let's take a look...

Love is patient, love is kind. It does not envy, it does not boast, it is not proud. It does not dishonor others, it is not self-seeking, it is not easily angered, it keeps no record of wrongs. It always protects, always trusts, always hopes, always perseveres. Love never fails. But where there are prophecies, they will cease; where there are tongues, they will be stilled; where there is knowledge, it will pass away. 1 Corinthians 13:4-5, 7-8 NIV

None of this comes easy, especially if we are dealing with people who have hurt us deeply and don't seem to care. One thing that I do know is that God wants us to love. The word love is Mission in the King James version of the Bible - 310 times. Seems important to me.

Today, tell someone that you love him/her and mean it!

February 12

All Things Are Possible

Jesus said unto him, If thou canst believe, all things are possible to him that believeth Mark 9:23 KJV

Sometimes, when faced with challenges, the word impossible keeps ringing in our head and our heart begins to fail us. We begin to think that we have the solution to our own problems. Or we began to look for the solution in other people or things like food, drugs, alcohol and sex. We lose our faith in God and begin to trust in ourselves, and that's why most times we continue to deal with the same problems over and over. Jesus wants us to trust in Him and delete the word impossible from our vocabulary. He can do all things; nothing is impossible to Him.

We are often faced with situations that seem impossible. We should not give up but rather believe that God can turn impossible situations around.

Today, encourage yourself. Be reminded that nothing is too hard for God.

Continue in Love

As the father hath loved me, so have I loved you: continue ye in my love. John 15:9 KJV

Love is the foundation of the Christian faith. It is the language of the Gospel. It was love that propelled God to give His only begotten Son. It is, therefore, not strange for Jesus to remind His disciples to continue in the same love.

Love is expressive, it is not passive; however, it requires sacrifice. Jesus, our perfect example, has shown us how much one can sacrifice to express love. He died for an undeserving mankind. Not everyone in the world has accepted His love, yet He still loves us.

We must forget about people's actions, reactions and attitude toward us and show them love. Jesus does not guarantee us that everyone we show love will reciprocate or that love should be shown to only those who deserve it. We must love even as God has loved us.

As you step out today, make a decision to continue speaking the language of love. A little text message or a phone call to check up on friends and family is enough to minister the love of God. Offer a smile, kind gesture or a kind word to strangers. It might make someone's day.

February 14

Live to Give

Give, and it shall be given unto you; good measure, pressed down, and shaken together, and running over, shall men give into your bosom. For with the same measure that ye mete withal it shall be measured to you again. Luke 6:38 KJV

I believe that God wants you to be happy. He is no respecter of persons. He wants the same for everyone. According to John 10:10, He wants us to live an abundant life, The thief cometh not, but for to steal, and to kill, and to destroy: I am come that they might have life, and that they might have it more abundantly. John 10:10 KJV.

As nurses, we give a part of ourselves to those we serve. We find true fulfillment when we give to others. God promises to multiply back to you what you give to others; knowing that whatsoever good thing any man doeth, the same shall he receive of the Lord, whether he be bond or free. Ephesians 6:8 KJV. The seeds you sow will produce a harvest in your life. God does not sleep. He sees all the good you are doing.

The purpose of your giving should not be to impress or prove something to others. When God blesses you, He has more than you in mind. Ask God to bless you so you can bless others.

February 15

The Lord Is My Guide

And the Lord, he it is that doth go before thee; he will be with thee, he will not fail thee, neither forsake thee: fear not, neither be dismayed. Deuteronomy 31:8 KJV

There is a new challenge every day. In life, there are so many twists and turns and ups and downs. We need a good guide to help us know which way to go. I love this scripture because it reminds me that God has gone before me and He is with me. That is good news.

As we are traveling down the road of life, we should not worry about where we are going. We should be concerned about who we are following. Some people have no idea where they are going. They are traveling haphazardly through life without any direction or guidance. Wouldn't you rather follow God's lead and stay on course?

Today, meditate on God's Word, ask the Lord to help you quickly obey Him and follow His leadership and ask the Lord to lead and guide you where He wants you to go.

February 16

In Love

And do everything with love. 1 Corinthians 16:14 NLT

Mentorship, partnering and collaboration are key to moving ahead in your life - personally, spiritually or professionally. Whether you are the giver or the receiver, do it all in love. Remember, you're not in love with everyone, but how you treat them should be with love, just like Jesus treats you. No matter what we do or who we come across, doing things in love makes everything more harmonious.

As we continue to care for one another and ourselves, we must love with the love of Christ. On your path, you will encounter challenging situations, circumstances and people. Ask yourself - what would Jesus do about that situation, circumstance or person? He would face a challenging situation with love. Keep love first in all that you do in life.

February 17

Know Love?

Dear friends, let us continue to love one another, for love comes from God. Anyone who loves is a child of God and knows God. But anyone who does not love does not know God for God is love.
1 John 4:8 NLT

What is love? The short answer is God. God is love. To know God is to know love. God's very being is love. His personality is love. As believers in Jesus Christ, we have the love of Jesus in us. As we face every day, the world should see the love of God in everything that we do. They should see it through our conduct, behavior and speech. When someone sees you, they should see the Love (God) that's deep in your soul.

As you go about day-to-day tasks, duties and lives, think about the love of Christ that dwells within you. As difficult as it may be at times, we must love one another as Christ has loved us.

Remember this, Love from the center of who you are; don't fake it. Run for dear life from evil; hold on for dear life to good. Be good friends who love deeply; practice playing second fiddle (Romans 12:9 MSG).

No Fear in Love

Such love has no fear, because perfect love expels all fear. If we are afraid, it is for fear or punishment, and this shows that we have not fully experienced his perfect love. 1 John 4:18 NLT

There is no need to fear your future. There are those in the world who would want you to be fearful of where you will spend eternity, or they want you to doubt that heaven really exists. But trust me, heaven is real. As believers in Jesus Christ, we are destined to see Jesus face-to-face when we leave this earth. There's no fear in knowing and loving God. If, for some strange reason, you are fearful, focus on the enormous amount of love God has for us, His children. Rest in knowing that you're in the palm of His hand for eternity.

John tells us in Chapter 17 that we cannot be plucked out of the hand of God. As long as you are abiding with Him, He will abide in you (John 15:4). There is no fear when we're resting in the loving arms of our Father in heaven.

Remember this, Be strong. Take courage. Don't be intimidated. Don't give them a second thought because God, your God, is striding ahead of you. He's right there with you. He won't let you down; he won't leave you (Deuteronomy 31:6 MSG).

February 19

Love for All

For God loved the world so much that he gave his one and only Son, so that everyone who believes in him will not perish but have eternal life. John 3:16 NLT

This passage is probably one of the most quoted bible verses. This verse shows God's agape love for all people. Agape love is unconditional love. We, as people, are conditional with our love. I love you if you do this; I love you if you get me this; I love you because… But God's love has no conditions attached to it. God gave us His best when He sent His son to live among us and to die on the cross for the sins of the world. There is no greater love than God's agape love.

As believers, we are to tell the world about the amazing love God has for His children. Wherever we go, and whoever we see as we go along life's journey, share the love of Jesus with the young, old, male or female. Everyone needs the love of Jesus in his/her life.

Reflect on this, Jesus said, "'Love the Lord your God with all your passion and prayer and intelligence.' This is the most Important, the first on any list. But there is a second to set alongside it: 'Love others as well as you love yourself.' These two commands are pegs; everything in God's Law and the Prophets hands from them."

God's Love is Beyond Measure

I am convinced that nothing can separate us from his love. Death can't, and life can't. The angels can't, and the demons can't. Our fears for today, our worries about tomorrow, and even the powers of hell can't keep God's love away. Whether we are high above the sky or in the deepest ocean, nothing in all creation will ever be able to separate us from the love of God that is revealed in Christ Jesus our Lord. Romans 8:38-39 NIV

Were you ever part of a wedding party? There is so much that goes along with that. The bride and groom select their dress and tuxedo. The bridesmaids and groomsmen try on their respective dresses and suits. But rarely are you able to pick something off the rack and it fits perfectly. You have to get fitted for it. The seamstress or tailor takes out his/her tape measure and begins to nip and tuck all the appropriate places. They tuck around the waist, the pant leg, the shoulders, etc. But the seamstress and tailor are limited on what he/she is able to do. He/she is limited based on the shape of the client and the amount of material he/she is working with. But God's love is beyond measure. There's nothing that limits God's love. God's love is everlasting. But what does that mean? Paul tells us in Romans 8:38-39: There is nothing here on earth or beyond earth that can separate us from the love of God. Death, nor life, fear, nor worry can get in between the love that God has for you. Nothing above and nothing below can interfere with God's love for you. When you're feeling low, remember - God still loves you, no matter what's going on in your life. There is nothing that can separate you from God's love, ABSOLUTELY NOTHING!

February 21

Power, Love, Sound Mind

For God has not given us a spirit of fear and timidity, but of power, love and self-discipline. 2 Timothy 1:7 NLT

Think back to a time in your life when you were asked to do something that was out of your comfort zone. Maybe it was your first lecture, speech or sermon. You were nervous and your hands were shaking. All you could do was say, "I studied this. Why am I so nervous?" That discomfort was God pushing you a step further in life to catapult you into greatness. Don't be afraid of where God is sending you or taking you. God has already prepared you for the task at hand. So, when that task or situation comes up again, remember - God imputed in you and to you, power, love and a sound mind. When you stand up, you're facing your fear. Stand tall and remember that God is with you. You got this and God has you.

Reflect on what the psalm writer says in Psalm 18:1 (MSG), I love you, God—you make me strong. God is bedrock under my feet, the castle in which I live, my rescuing knight. My God—the high crag where I run for dear life, hiding behind the boulders, safe in the granite hideout.

True Friendship

There is no greater love than to lay down one's life for one's friends. John 15:13 NLT

Who's your best friend…your spouse, mom, dad, friend? Would you die for them? I know we often say it…but do we really mean it? Really mean it? True friendship displays love and forgiveness. True friendship allows you to call a "spade a spade" when things go awry. True friendship embraces the person but condemns the sin. True friendship brings the wayward friend back into the fold of love for Jesus. Proverbs 17:9 (NLT) reminds us that love prospers when a fault is forgiven, but dwelling on it separates close friends. When we think about friendship, we must look at it through the lens of our Savior, Jesus. Jesus displayed the ultimate love when He died on the cross for the sins of the world. Clearly, there is no greater love than a friend who would lay down his/her life for another.

As you go about your day today, reflect on what is told to us in Proverbs 17:17 (MSG), Friends love through all kinds of weather, and families stick together in all kinds of trouble.

First Love

We love each other because he loved us first. 1 John 4:19 NLT

Do you remember your first love? The one that made you giggle or smile whenever he/she called you on the phone? I see you smiling now as you begin to think about it. That first true love of a potential mate made you warm all over. You couldn't wait until you saw or spoke to him/her again. Whether it was "puppy love," teenage bliss or love after 50, it's the type of love that one never forgets.

The love that John is speaking about in 1 John 4:19 is agape love. In other words, it's an unconditional love. As a believer in Christ, we are to seek God's unconditional love for our fellow brothers and sisters. God's love seeks love. God's love demonstrates love. As you go about your day today, show someone the love of God.

Think about this, My dear children, let's not just talk about love; let's practice real love. This is the only way we'll know we're living truly, living in God's reality. It's also the way to shut down debilitation self-criticism, even when there is something to it. For God is greater than our worried hearts and knows more about us than we do ourselves (1 John 3:18 MSG).

February 24

Perfect Harmony

Above all, clothe yourselves with love, which binds us all together in perfect harmony. Colossians 3:14 NLT

Is there anything in life that is harmonious? In our human minds, we would say no. We'd say no, because, as humans, we don't always get along with one another. But in Colossians, the Apostle Paul tells us that we are to wrap ourselves with love. That love is the love of Jesus. When we have the love of Jesus in our hearts, we can forgive those that offend us. When we have the love of Jesus, we can face those who despitefully use us. When we have the love of Jesus, we can face anything that crosses our path. When we all have the love of Jesus in our hearts, we can work in perfect harmony.

As you think about ways to live in harmony with those in your life, read and reflect on Acts 2:43 (MSG), Everyone around was in awe—all those wonders and signs done through the apostles! And all the believers lived in a wonderful harmony, holding everything in common. They sold whatever they owned and pooled their resources so that each person's need we met.

February 25

Love One Another

So now I am giving you a new commandment: Love each other. Just as I have loved you, you should love each other. Your love for another will prove to the world that you are my disciples. John 13:34-35 NLT

Jesus gave us clear instructions. We are to love one another. That's challenging, especially when we feel that we have been wronged or hurt. But when we have been wronged or hurt, that is the perfect time to show love. You can show love by how you respond to the offense. You can show love by being the one to extend the olive branch first. When we love one another, even those who have offended us, we show that we are a follower of Christ.

One might ask, how can I show love if the person isn't ready or willing to hear? That's a good question, and there's no simple answer. Each person is different. I encourage you to pray about the situation or circumstances and ask God to give you the words to say or the action to take. At the end of the day, we are to love one another as Christ has instructed us to do. What would Jesus do in your situation? Simply put, love one another.

February 26

Steadfast Love

But you, O Lord, are a God of compassion and mercy,
slow to get angry and filled with unfailing love and
faithfulness. Psalms 86:15 NLT

Have you shown compassion and mercy to anyone lately? Compassion is to show sympathy for the mishaps or misfortunes of others. For example, one would show compassion towards those who are sick in nursing homes or hospitals, or someone dying from a disease. We show them care and concern as we interact with them.

God exudes compassion and mercy towards us every day. To know God is to understand that there is no love like the love of God. When the world feels like it is crashing down around you, the presence of God's love is comforting. God's steadfast love protects us, just as a parent would protect his/her child. God's love is consistent and steadfast. It doesn't waiver, although we may waiver. God shows us grace and mercy - every day of our lives. We should take a page out of God's word, and be slow to anger and be filled with forgiveness and love.

The psalm writer was eloquent when he said in Psalm 136:23 (MSG), God remembered us when we were down, His love never quits. Rescued us from the trampling boot, His love never quits. Takes care of everyone in time of need. His love never quits. Thank God, who did it all! His love never quits!

February 27

God Loves Us

But God is so rich in mercy, and he loved us so much, that even though we were dead because of our sins, he gave us life when he raised Christ from the dead. (It is only by God's grace that you have been saved!) Ephesians 2:4-5 NLT

There are times in our lives when we wonder if we are liked, let alone loved. We wonder, "If I do this, will they like me?" or "If I buy them this, will they love me?" The best feeling to have is to know that God loves YOU! Every inch of you; every flaw you can find, God still loves you.

God knew about us before the foundation of the world. He knew that our sinful ways would separate us from Him permanently if a solution were not found. The solution came in the form of Jesus Christ dying on the cross over 2,000 years ago. Christ dying on the cross and rising from the dead gave us life and love. Life to live with Him forever and love to cover a multitude of sins. Dearly beloved, know that God still loves you, despite your sinful nature. Embrace His love today.

I'm so glad that "God loves all who hate evil, and those who love him he keeps safe, snatches them from the grip of the wicked" (Psalm 97:10 MSG). What an amazing God we serve.

Sincere Love

Don't just pretend to love others. Really love them. Hate what is wrong. Hold tightly to what is good. Love each other with genuine affection, and take delight in honoring each other. Romans 12:9-10 NLT

Fake. Phony. Shallow. All these words can describe how someone can "love" someone else. The Apostle Paul says that we should not pretend to love other people. The "fake it to you make it" method to love isn't Christ-like. We are to love others not to fake love. The challenge is to love a person and to hate the sin. We all fall short of where we should be in our various forms of relationships. Our responsibility as believers is to correct our fallen brothers or sisters in love. We're not to hold their sin over their head and hold them hostage. We are to truly and sincerely love them just as Christ loves us. We must remember that despite how we treat God, He sincerely loves us. Just as God shows us love, we, too, are to show others true and genuine love.

Think on these things: So this is my prayer: that your love will flourish and that you will not only love much but well. Learn to love appropriately. You need to use your head and test your feelings so that your love is sincere and intelligent, not sentimental gush. Live a lover's life, circumspect and exemplary, a life Jesus will be proud of: bountiful in fruits from the soul, making Jesus Christ attractive to all, getting everyone involved in the glory and praise of God. Philippians 1:9 MSG

March Health Awareness

Multiple Sclerosis Education and Awareness

National Bleeding Disorder Awareness

National Colorectal Cancer Awareness

National Endometriosis Awareness

National Kidney Month

National Traumatic Brain Injury Awareness

March 1

Survival

I pray that God, the source of hope, will fill you completely with joy and peace because you trust in him. Then you will overflow with confident hope through the power of the Holy Spirit. Romans 15:13 NLT

Heavy hearts are the result of life's daily stresses and worry. Widespread evil and violence can drain your spirit. Do not be discouraged and do not be afraid. God is your source. He can bring you peace and joy in the midst of chaos. Build your confident and hope in Him. Lean on your faith and trust in God's plan as they are also vital elements that will help pull you through trying times. Ensure that you make prayer a habit for it plays an instrumental role in your survival. What you are going through does not come as a surprise to God. He allows things like this to happen to get you to reaffirm your trust in His will. Every blessing, lesson, test, trial, tribulation, and message is orchestrated by the Father. Take solace in knowing that nothing happens without His permission. If He has allowed something to happen, rest assured that He has already pre-equipped you to handle it. Stand on His word for you are a Survivor!

Reclaim Your Mind

My soul, wait thou only upon God; for my expectation is from him.
Psalm 62:5 KJV

Trying to anticipate what the day or the future brings will cause interruptions in your peace. It may consume your thoughts and paralyze your ability to focus. As you fill your mind with anticipation and worry about those things that are beyond your control, you rob yourself of the ability to see the blessings that you have been allowed to enjoy in this life. Anxiety builds and sometimes is accompanied by depression. The constant torment of your mind does not make anything better, yet it tends to drain you. Pray without ceasing and free yourself from unnecessary apprehension. Concentrate and recenter your thoughts on the one who can bring you through each moment. Never lose sight of God's presence and your mind will rest easy in the reassurance of his everlasting love. Be at ease as you seek God's counsel and bask in His goodness and mercy. Allow Him to bear all your concerns. He can handle far more than you can. He is willing to bear these burdens if you let Him. Declutter your mind, refocus, and reclaim it then expect God to bring clarity and peace for you today and beyond.

Fear Not

For to be carnally minded is death; but to be spiritually minded is life and peace. Romans 8:6 KJV

There is a war constantly ensuing for control of your mind. The enemy would have you carnally minded with only thoughts of selfishness and rebellion against the law of God. He knows that you have been left weak and vulnerable from years of mental and emotional lamenting, so he tries to keep you in bondage and away for God's teachings, away from His presence. There is no need to fret for the enemy has no power over you. God is with you always and he will not let you die. His word reassures you that there is truly no need to fear anything as He is your courage and your strength. Refuge can be found in His arms. God encompasses your every thought and orders your every step. Be vigilant in constantly standing guard over your thoughts and remain in constant communication with the Father. God's spirit is alive and well within you therefore you must not become overwhelmed with the things of this world. Pray fervently and ask Him to guard your mind, body, soul, and spirit. He will give you peace, blessings, and abundant life.

March 4

Against All Odds

But I have trusted in thy mercy, my heart shall rejoice in thy salvation. I will sing unto the Lord, because he hath dealt bountifully with me. Psalm 13: 5-6 KJV

You have allowed the troubles of yesterday to creep back into your spirit. Your future looks uncertain and the odds seem stacked against you, but God. You should rejoice and shout from the mountain tops as He is the way-maker upon which your trust and faith should always remain in. Each step you take, situation & circumstance you face today is nothing to God. He will be your light in darkest days if you let Him. God can use you to be that same light in the darkness of the sick and shut-in patient, friend or family member that are suffering. Trust in His mercy and His grace. He is a comforter, provider, healer and much more. Maintain your faith against all the seemingly impossible odds that challenge and test you today. You are perfectly positioned for God to work on your behalf. You're right where you should be so keep your eyes steadfast on Him, never turn away from God, and in the end, you will ALWAYS beat all odds.

March 5

Laugh It Off

A merry heart doeth good like a medicine; but a broken spirit drieth the bones. Proverbs 17:22 KJV

So many things in this world can distract you and redirect your focus. You forget about the blessings and subconsciously begin to obsess over problems. But why are you so serious? Why do you take life and circumstances so seriously? Free yourself from the obsession of trying to solve everything on your own. That is not your job plus it's beyond your control anyway. Relax and let God handle everything for you. Your shoulders are not strong enough to carry life's burdens, but He is equipped and qualified to turn things around. Learn to laugh at yourself and your circumstances for a cheerful heart is like medicine for your soul. Your joy-filled laughter is like music to God's ears. It takes your focus off issues and lifts your spirit. Laughter lightens life's burdens and results in a positive outlook. Trust God to carry your burdens. He will do it if you simply give them to Him and allow Him to carry your load. So, laugh louder, enjoy His presence, and find peace in knowing He is with you always.

March 6

Draw Near

Let your light so shine before me, that they may see your good works, and glorify your Father which is in heaven.
Matthew 5:16 KJV

Today you are a magnet. People flock to you for advice, guidance, and simply want to be in your presence. Your radiant kindness and compassion have become a light in the darkness for the masses. Embrace it but do not become arrogant. For arrogance would not be God's will for you nor is it a becoming quality for God's servants. Remain humble and do not make the mistake of taking credit for what is happening. It is not you that people are drawn to but God's spirit that is radiating from you. Your connection to Him is shining so brightly that others look at you and see His image. This causes God's people to draw near you therefore you must draw even closer to Him. Stay focused on Him, what He wants you to say or do for His people and allow His radiance to be the light house today. You are the vessel He is using to bless His people so ensure you represent the Kingdom well. God's love is on display so let it illuminate through you and continue to draw God's people nearer to Him.

March 7

Don't Rush

Enthusiasm without knowledge is no good; haste makes mistakes.
Proverbs 19:2 NLT

The hustle and bustle of each day can be mindboggling. It can cause half-hearted efforts in all that you do as you rush through each task. You find yourself doing a lot yet finishing nothing and the mistakes made can sometimes be irreversible. Slow down and stop rushing through life missing out on God's lessons and blessings. Your hurriedness causes unstable and disorganized thoughts. You cannot continue to move in this way and expect your endurance to last. You will burnout and fail. Make the effort now, to carve out a time to put your FULL, undivided attention on God. Embrace Him as he showers you with His unconditional love and affection. This time with Him should never be rushed. Giving Him that sacred time and making Him a priority in your day is the best way to build a true relationship with Him. This time with God is not for Him but it's for you. He will bless you with instructions that will help you through your daily life. Spending time with the Father is a minor investment that yields major returns. Isn't He worth it?

March 8

Seek Him First

But seek ye first the kingdom of God, and his righteousness; and all these things shall be added unto you. Matthew 6:33 KJV

You have given your best efforts, but your goals continue to elude you. You have planned, saved, researched, and talked to everybody but you failed to do the one thing that changes everything…Pray! Why not? Did you forget where your help comes from? Why haven't you to talked to God yet? Whenever there is a decision to be made, you must seek God's counsel. Stop trying to do things without Him. You must always remember that anything that has not been ordained by the Father will not succeed. If you exclude Him, you will cause yourself hardship, delays, and ultimately, you will fail miserably. Remember to depend on Him and His guidance instead of leaning to your own understanding. Seek His stamp of approval. If you seek Him first in all that you do, He will provide all your needs. God can make the impossible possible. You have tried your way, now try God.

Attitude of Gratitude

This is the day that the Lord has made; We will rejoice and be glad in it. Psalm 118:24 NKJV

The attitude you began today with, should be one of gratitude as you are reminded that each day is a gift from God. It was not promised nor was it earned. You did nothing to deserve it. God loves you so much that He gave you another opportunity to live. Worship Him, rejoice and give thanks. Allow your heart to be open to appreciate this precious gift of life. Lift your voice and draw nearer to Him as you sing His praises. You are afforded one more chance to honor God with your love, kindness, and compassion for His people. Now thank Him for this day and the opportunity to get it right and make a positive impact on the lives of the patients you serve, the people you come in contact with, and your friends and family. Let your newfound attitude of gratitude shine through. Now, Go make this day GREAT!

March 10

He's On-Duty

For the LORD thy God will hold thy right hand, saying unto thee, Fear not, I will help thee. Isaiah 41:13 KJV

The Lord your God which goeth before you, he shall fight for you, according to all that he did for you in Egypt before your eyes. Deuteronomy 1: 30

While you were asleep, God was working. Preparations were being made for a successful day filled with blessings and new mercies. Keep calm and stay connected to Him as you move about your day. There is no need to worry or wonder what lies ahead. Just know that God has already made provisions for every circumstance. He has gone before you and cleared your path. He has made every crooked place straight, he will bring every high thing low, and He is making intercessions just for you. Your continuous communication with Him with help you through this day. He will not let anything overwhelm you and He will not let you fall. Focus on your blessings for they far outweigh your problems. God is with you! Remember, He will never leave you nor forsake you. He is always on-duty!

March 11

Eyes on The Prize

Counsel is mine, and sound wisdom; I am understanding, I have strength. Proverbs 8:14 NKJV

Life is not perfect, and things may not always go the way you think they should. You may be dealing with regrets, resentment, or strongholds of comparison. The opinions of others cause self-doubt. Do not let these things hold you captive. Do not allow them to clutter your mind or separate you from God. Remember, God has already taken into account the wrong turns and mistakes that you've made. Stop beating yourself up and accept His new mercies that are available to you every morning. Instead, be confident in knowing that God has everything you need. Always remember that He knew you before you were formed in your mother's womb. He had a plan and a purpose for your life. If you fix your thoughts on Him, rely on your God-given insight and not your eyesight, you will be amazed at the peace you will gain. Now go out, make today memorable and always keep your eyes on the prize!

March 12

Take Refuge

God is our refuge and strength, a very present help in trouble.
Psalm 46:1 KJV

Unexpected things happen and can cause overwhelming stress, anxiety, and depression. You battle within yourself and rely on your own strength to overcome these mental and emotional burdens, the internal and external turmoil. You feel powerless and do not know how you will continue to go on. These battles are not yours and you are not equipped to battle them solo. God is readily available to fight for you and bring calm to your mind and soul if you would ask Him. He promises to walk with you through all life's trials, but you have to go to Him in prayer and make your request known. Return to Him for guidance and allow Him in. He is your refuge and your present help in times of trouble. God wants to hear your heart's desires. He wants you to lay out your request before Him and trust Him. When you take refuge in God, you are fully trusting that He will take care of you and make you feel safe and secure. He will provide all that you need to endure life's challenges. There is nothing too big for God. He loves you and will make sure that everything will always be alright! Believe in His word and have no doubts.

March 13

Ask God

Ask, and it will be given to you; seek, and you will find; knock, and it will be opened to you. For everyone who asks receives, and he who seeks finds, and to him who knocks it will be opened. Matthew 7:7-8 NKJV

Is there anything too hard for God? You hesitate to ask for the things you need and desire. You constantly try to figure everything out on your own. Why do you continue to do this to yourself? Have you not learned yet? God wants you to come to Him with your requests. Ask Him for your heart's desires. He already knows what your needs and desires are before you ever ask. Remember what the scripture says in Matthew 7:7 "Ask, and it shall be given you; seek, and ye shall find; knock, and it shall be opened unto you." If you choose not to make your requests known, then you choose to go without. Simply ask God for exactly what you need; but remember to thank Him for all He has already done. You may not be sure what you should ask for but ask God to help you figure things out. Ask Him to help you reach your personal and professional goals. Take solace in knowing that your request does not have to be articulated with eloquence or sophistication. There is no need to dress it up. Simply ask. Asking Him is not selfish, it is actually exercising your faith. You show God that you believe in His word, His ability to provide and you trust Him to do so. He is waiting for you! Pray about everything but do not worry about anything. Take heed to God's word and always remember to simply ask.

March 14

Complain No More

Now when the people complained, it displeased the LORD; for the LORD heard it and His anger was aroused. So the fire of the LORD burned among them, and consumed some in the outskirts of the camp. Numbers 11:1 NKJV

Complaining about your situation today will not fix it. It will not cause your job to be more rewarding, your children to be more respectful, your bills to be paid, nor your relationship to be perfect. No, complaining only takes your focus off the important things, your blessings. When you complain, it takes you to a place filled with negativity and ungratefulness. So why do it? Instead, try looking at your situation and acknowledging the blessings that you have. Start rejoicing and praising God for what He has already done and delivered you from. Praise God for your health and strength. For the food on your table, clothes on your back, roof over your head, job that you have (and someone else is praying for) and your family that loves you. See, praise invokes a special kind of response from God. Your praise is a great way to show gratitude and return your focus onto Him. No more complaining, only praise!

March 15

Past Lessons

There is therefore now no condemnation to those who are in Christ Jesus…And we know that all things work together for good to those who love God, to those who are the called according to His purpose. Romans 8:1a, 28 NKJV

You are not feeling it today and you are consumed with thoughts of past failures. They haunt you and cause you to doubt your ability to move forward. Why are you giving your past so much power over your present and future? God wants you to trust Him in these moments. Do not let your past cost you the purpose that God has for you. Ask Him to help you work through your doubt. Instead of torturing yourself with the past, focus on today and forgive yourself for yesterday's mistakes. If you continue looking in the rear-view mirror of your life, you will miss out on the beauty and blessings you have today. Always be reminded that God has a plan and purpose for your life. Take the lessons from those past experiences and let God's blessings shine through. Remember all things work together for your good.

March 16

Reassurance

Delight yourself also in the Lord; and He shall give you the desires of your heart. Psalm 37:4 NKJV

Your focus should be on Jesus daily which makes it easier to face each challenge. Take the time to seek His presence and avoid distractions that try to steer you away from Him. Daily communion with you is one of His great delights. Remember, consistency and daily conversations are required to develop a true relationship with Him. In return, He will provide the desires of your heart and unexplainable peace in the midst of your internal storms. He will never let you down nor will He leave to fight any battles alone. Praise Him in every season for every reason. Be assured and know that He is your anchor, hope, strength, and foundation. Remind yourself daily that God is faithful, ever-present, and His word never returns to you void. Delight yourself in Him, stand firm on His promises with full assurance of His commitment to you, and know that all is truly well. Now bless His holy name, rejoice, and go be a blessing to your patients.

March 17

Treasures

Do not store up for yourselves treasures on earth, where moths and vermin destroy, and where thieves break in and steal. But store up for yourselves treasures in heaven, where moths and vermin do not destroy, and where thieves do not break in and steal. For where your treasure is, there your heart will be also.
Matthew 6:19-21 NIV

Where does treasures lie? In material things, your job, money? These things are temporary, have no substance, and no return on your investment. However, if you invest in your spiritual growth, affirming your trust in God, you build equity in Him. You will feel an increased compounded interest and desire to be close to Him. You become more confident and empowered as your relationship with Him flourishes. In those times of trouble, this unbreakable bond with God will sustain you and raging storms will no longer be able to overtake you. Store your treasures up in heaven by constantly depositing God in your spirit and investing quality time with Him into your daily life. The return will be worth it!

March 18

Equipped and Qualified

Be on guard. Stand firm in the faith. Be courageous. Be strong.
1 Corinthians 16:13 NLT

Today's challenges may cause you to question your strength and courage. It may test your faith and leave you feeling bond and hopeless. It is at times like these that you must remember to be steadfast and unmovable. Trust in God and His process. Do not doubt the word and purpose He has for your life. He has already equipped you with everything you need to face each obstacle. Your victory was predestined before you were born. Allow God to intercede on your behalf and remember, your success is guaranteed. He has qualified you with a special skill set that makes you a prime candidate for today's tasks. Embrace it, keep your faith strong, trust His plan, and follow His guidance. God remains in control. You are perfectly equipped and qualified for anything this day brings. Hold on to His unchanging hand, stand on His word, and go make a difference in someone's life today. Everything you need is within you!

March 19

Love Without Limits

Love is patient, love is kind. It does not envy, it does not boast, it is not proud. It does not dishonor others, it is not self-seeking, it is not easily angered, it keeps no record of wrongs. Love does not delight in evil but rejoices with the truth. It always protects, always trusts, always hopes, always perseveres. Love never fails 1 Corinthians 13:4-8b NIV

The word of God reminds us that love is patient, kind, and keeps no records of wrongs. Remind yourself of this confirmation as you embark on your daily walk with God. Hatred displayed by others can easily consume you and cause you to respond negatively or retaliate. This would not be God's way. Do not allow someone else's actions or words to deter you from putting God's love on display. He calls us to love in spite of; to love unconditionally. God has loved you even when you were lost in sin. If He loves you without limitations, through your good and bad decisions, attitudes, and actions. Is it not fitting to return this to others? Today, allow His unconditional, love to beam through you as you care for your patients. Remember, His love is everlasting, and limitless so represent well today.

March 20

Enhance and Shine

You are the salt of the earth. But if the salt loses its' saltiness, how can it be made salty again? It is no longer good for anything, except to be thrown out and trampled underfoot. You are the light of the world. A town built on a hill cannot be hidden. Neither do people light a lamp nor put it under a bowl. Instead they put it on its stand, and it gives light to everyone in the house. In the same way, let your light shine before others, that they may see your good deeds and glorify your Father in heaven. Matthew 5:13-16 NIV

Each time you walk into a room you bring a certain aura. Your glow draws others near. According to God's Word, you are the salt of the earth. This means that you preserve and enhance everything and everyone you come in contact with. You bring comfort, compassion, and kindness with your mere presence. You bring flavor to this bland world. God has strategically placed you in your current situation and position to be an enhancement to His people; to guide them out of their darkness with the light He has placed inside you. Today, strive to continue to let your light shine so bright that it forges the way for others to reach Christ. He is waiting for you.

March 21

Lead the Way

Kings take pleasure in honest lips; they value the one who speaks what is right. Proverbs 16:13 NIV

It is said that in order to be a good leader, you must first be a good follower. You should be able to follow directions as well as you are able to give them. Inspiring others to follow instructions and empowering team members/co-workers to put their best efforts into whatever project they are working on helps you lead properly. A good leader should also be fair and just with rewards and punishments. As you embark upon your day, reflect upon the character of God and follow his leadership example. Humble yourself and make sure your God-given leadership skills are representing Him well. Remember He desires to orders your steps and shows you the correct path throughout this day. Allow His commandments to be your foundation, follow them, then live according to His will and His word. Always ensure your moral principles and character are a true reflection of His guidance. Show yourself worthy of being followed by leading by example, with love, honesty, and integrity. Allow God to be the blueprint for your daily decisions and actions. He is the ultimate Leader and is waiting to use you to lead the way and guide His people towards Him.

March 22

Timing Is Everything

To everything there is a season, and a time to every purpose under the heaven. Ecclesiastes 3:1 KJV

Today you are rushing and hurrying along. You feel the need for immediate resolutions to problems. You want a microwave answer for a crock pot issue. You expect instant gratification from the time you have invested then become overwhelmed and anxious when you experience a delay. Be reminded that anything gained quickly will not last. It will fade just as quickly as it is obtained. Remember there is no elevator to any form of success, you have to take the stairs. Instead, seek to enjoy the process without the burden of hurrying toward the finished product of your efforts. Tune-in to the lessons God is revealing to you along your path and be determined to gain wisdom for each of them. Always remember, nothing happens until God ordains it. Despite your expectations or desire for speedy conclusions, everything is according to God's timing only. He is always on time and His timing is perfect.

March 23

Let Go and Let God

Jesus Christ the same yesterday, and today, and forever.
Hebrews 13:8 KJV

Admitting things are beyond your control is not an easy feat. There are people depending on you to make things happen in a timely fashion. You are expected to work miracles in the most impossible circumstances. This happens in many aspects of your life but at some point, you realize that you cannot do everything, and nothing is truly within your control. It is time to learn to let go. Let go of those things that cause you grief, anxiety, worry, and emotional turmoil. Let go of negative situations and negative people. Let go of control. It is time to let go and let God have His way. Rest in the assurance of His abundance and magnificent presence. Rest now is His security and constant peace. As soon as you relinquish your control and release all your cares to Him, God can begin His work. Get out of His way and allow Him to take care of you just as He has before.

March 24

Beyond What You Can See

So we fix our eyes not on what is seen, but on what is unseen,
since what is seen is temporary, but what is unseen is eternal.
2 Corinthians 4:18 NIV

When you choose to change your perspective, you choose to change your entire life. Today is the perfect day to try seeing things through God's lens. While you are only capable of seeing in the physical realm, He is able to see things spiritually. So, who has a clearer view? Of course, He does. Remember, when you start to look at things through God's eyes, from His perspective, you realize that the things that you have allowed to consume your focus are really minuscule and unimportant. Shake it off. Take your power back. Do not waste any more of your valuable time on invaluable thoughts or negative people. Instead, turn your focus back to God. He will fill your hearts with unspeakable joy, forgiveness, humility, and thanksgiving; filling your life with peace beyond understanding. Look beyond what your eyes can see and start looking at everything with a renewed Godly perspective. As you enter your day, ask the Lord to allow you see people through His eyes and expect your life to change for the better. You will no longer see the external but instead you will see their hearts just as God sees them.

March 25

Servant's Heart

In your relationships with one another, have the same mindset as Christ Jesus: Who, being in very nature God, did not consider equality with God something to be used to his own advantage; rather, he made himself nothing by taking the very nature of a servant, being made in human likeness. And being found in appearance as a man, he humbled himself by becoming obedient to death—even death on a cross! Philippians 2:5-8 NIV

Being a servant requires humility which can be elusive to some but a natural skill for others. Jesus Himself took on the servant role when He washed the feet of His disciples. To be like Him, you must follow His example and His lead to ensure you will be blessed. Move today with a servant's heart. Remove yourself from selfish thoughts and actions. For selfishness is not of God. Embrace humility, kindness, and recognize who you are in relationship with God. Lend a helping hand to others as He has done so many times for you. Expose any prideful ways that you are harboring and ask God to help you become more like Him in your daily walk. He will guide you to realign with His will and put you on the path toward His glory.

March 26

Controlled Resentment

Search me, O God, and know my heart: try me, and know my thoughts: And see if there be any wicked way in me, and lead me in the way everlasting. Psalm 139:23-24 KJV

When trouble stirs up in your life or things do not go as planned, your response is important. You may become disappointed or resentful. You may be angry as you were unable to dictate or control the outcomes. You may even question God and His motives for not allowing things to come to pass according to your desires. Who are you to question God? He does not owe you anything. Everything that you have, God gave it to you, and He was not obligated to do so. Those were gifts so govern yourself appropriately. Do not present yourself as an entitled brat. Instead, ask God to help you expose your resentments and assist you with them. Praise Him for what He has given you, unseen dangers that He has protected you from, and for His influence in your life. He knows what lies ahead and what is best for you. Trust Him!

March 27

In His Presence

Lord, the God of Israel, there is no God like you in heaven above or on earth below – you who keep your covenant of love with your servants who continue wholeheartedly in your way. 1 Kings 8:23 NIV

Commune with God today. Let your worries disappear as you bask in His presence. Communicate your needs, concerns, and goals but be reminded that you are exactly where you are supposed to be. He will prepare you privately for your purpose then allow it to bloom in public. You will bear great fruit if you simply stay close to God. In Him you are privileged to develop an everlasting relationship that will richly enhance every aspect of your life. There is no one more important than Him. Peace and joy will be your reward. Trust and believe in Him. Today, ask God to go with you everywhere you go. As you care for patients, ask Him to be with you and guide your hand. Remember, God is omnipresent; He is always there.

March 28

Constantly Thankful

In every thing give thanks: for this is the will of God in
Christ Jesus concerning you. 1 Thessalonians 5:18

Be overflowing with thankfulness as you enter into your day. Open your eyes to see the riches and glory of God. Look around as you inhale the breath of life that was gifted to you with this morning's sunrise. Listen to the sounds of God's creatures and be reminded of His splendor. Even in difficult circumstances, remember, God wants to bring good out of every situation. That does not mean that things will be good at all times. It means that all things will work out for your good in the long run. Isn't it amazing to know that God is working in the shadows to ensure an ultimately victorious outcome? Acknowledge His constant presence and sing His praises. Always be mindful that your praise invokes power and healing, and it is therapeutic to your soul. Today, as you care for your patients, encourage each of them to hold to God's promises and inspire them to adopt an attitude of gratitude. Remind each of them about God's unconditional love, grace, mercy, and healing power. Help them to center their thoughts on God, allowing thankfulness and praise to become priority in their lives then watch His blessings overflow abundantly. Remember, give thanks in everything.

March 29

Don't Be Deceived

The eternal God is your refuge, And underneath are the everlasting arms. Deuteronomy 33:27a NKJV

Beware of self-destructive behaviors and thoughts that drive you toward temptations. Negative conversations and gossip are tools of the enemy and reveal weakness of your flesh. Do not waste your precious time and energy engaging in these deceptive behaviors. Instead, recognize them as tricks of Satan and fight against it. Remember, Satan's job is to steal, kill, and destroy. He will attack you from every angle and manipulate you if you do not stay rooted and ground in God's word. Keep your guards up and do not be deceived. Challenge this evil and it will flee from you. Regain control of yourself and surrender fully to the Lord. This is a perfect opportunity to gain strength in God's arms, in His presence. Be of good courage and know that God will fight your battles on your behalf. Run to Him for guidance as you resist the deceiver. Look to Him for all your needs and rejoice in His abundance. He is with you always! He will never leave you or forsake you. He is your refuge, strength, and a present help in times of trouble.

March 30

His Favor

He said, "If I have found favor in your eyes, my lord, do not pass your servant by. Genesis 18:3 NIV

You feel inadequate and unworthy when mistakes are made. Somehow you have deceived yourself into believing that God's love is predicated on your performance but that is not the case. You have God's favor. His favor can be granted at any time and it is available to anyone. Remember God has no respect of person and what He does for one, He will do for you. The bible tells us that God's favor will open doors and make possible what seems impossible. Understand that there is absolutely nothing that can separate you from His love. Do not allow the enemy to convince you with his lies. Do not believe that God would leave you based on your behavior. His love is not attributed to your actions and you did nothing to earn it. His love and favor are unconditional gifts that will engulf your heart with a pleasant reassurance. As you begin your shift today, pray God's favor over your patients and all those you are charged to care for. Remember, His favor can change any situation, heal any illness, and restore anything in a blink of an eye. Return to your knowledge of Him as it transforms, restores, and cleanses your soul. Maintain purity in your heart and open yourself completely to His presence as He uses you to care for His people today. He loves you more than you can ever imagine and know that you have His favor over your life!

March 31

No Doubt

According as he hath chosen us in him before the foundation of the world, that we should be holy and without blame before him in love. Ephesians 1:4 KJV

Self-doubt can steal your joy and peace. It can make you question your worth and place limits on your motivation. Do not allow this trick of the enemy to deceive you. Remember, you are a child of the Most High and if you trust Him and His plan, you will be successful. Your path and purpose in this life was chosen long before the world was created. God designed you to walk with Him through each moment as He orders your every step. Focus your energy on building a relationship with God instead of trying to anticipate your future. God's plans are for your prosperity, not for harm to befall you. As you care for your patients today, remember that God is with you and by your side. He will guide your every decision, speak through you, and use your hands to heal His people. Ask God to remove any doubts from your mind about your ability to carry out your assignments. Allow Him to take control and ask for guidance as you move through your day. Let your care, compassion, and kindness be on display as you work without doubt, with boldness, and confidence. Remember that God chose you for this noble role and He had no doubt in your ability for success. Trust His decision to place you here, relinquish all doubts then your peace and joy will forever be plentiful.

April Health Awareness

Alcohol Awareness

National Autism Awareness

National Child Abuse Prevention

National Sarcoidosis Awareness

Oral Cancer Awareness

Sexual Assault Awareness and Prevention

Sexually Transmitted Disease Awareness Month

National Public Health Week (April 6-12)

World Health Day (April 7)

National Infertility Awareness Week (April 19-25)

April 1

You Are A Testimony

The woman left her water jar beside the well and ran back to the village, telling everyone, "Come and see a man who told me everything I ever did!" John 4:28-29a NLT

As I think about my life, I can say that I have a testimony. As believers in Christ, we all have a testimony. He has truly been with you through your good times and bad times. Although my life is not yours, and yours is not mine, we all have had troubles in our lives that we may or may not have dealt well with. The Apostle Paul was a self-titled, chief persecutor of early Christians. But as he was traveling one day, God covered his eyes with scales and blinded him (The Book of Acts). But after his conversion, God lifted the scales from his eyes, and instead of becoming a chief persecutor, he became a chief witness of Jesus Christ. Paul could say, that through all that he had done, God did not destroy him but spared his life in order that he could tell the world about Jesus. Through all that you've been through, know that with faith in Christ, you too can become an excellent witness for Him through your testimony.

What does your testimony say about you? By an act of faith, Enoch skipped death completely, "They looked all over and couldn't find him because God had taken him." We know on the basis of reliable testimony that before he was taken "he pleased God." It's impossible to please God apart from faith. And why? Because anyone who wants to approach God must believe both that he exists and that he cares enough to respond to those who seek him. Hebrews 11:5 MSG

April 2

Just A Little Talk with Jesus

Never stop praying. 1 Thessalonians 5:17 NLT

When was the last time you "ran away" to be with God for any length of time? Some of us may never have had true time alone with God. What I mean by this is simple: We all need time away from everything and everyone to hear from God. This doesn't have to cost a lot of money. You don't necessarily have to go on a retreat, but simply go to the nearest park and take a walk or sit beside the lake or river and just talk to God. There are plenty of examples in the Bible where people got away from others to speak to God. Moses often separated himself from others in order to hear from God (Exodus 8:30, Exodus 19:20-23:33). Jesus also escaped from the crowd to reconnect with God (Matt. 14:23, Mark 6:46, Luke 6:12). The question of the day is this: Do you plan on getting away to hear from God any time soon? He's waiting to talk to you.

Are you willing to talk to Him? Make this your common practice: Confess your sins to each other and pray for each other so that you can live together whole and healed. The prayer of a person living right with God is something powerful to be reckoned with. Elijah, for instance, human just like us, prayed hard that it wouldn't rain, and it didn't—not a drop for three and a half years. Then he prayed that it would rain, and it did. The showers came and everything started growing again. James 5:16 MSG

April 3

Roadblocks

Seek the Kingdom of God above all else, and live righteously, and he will give you everything you need. Matthew 6:33 NLT

Roadblocks, obstacles and hurdles all deter us from getting to our destination. My question to you is simple: Are you a roadblock for God's blessings? There are many examples throughout the scripture that show how people have been a roadblock to their own blessings; for example, there is Adam and Eve (Genesis Chapters 1-3), David (2 Samuel Chapters 11 & 12) and Jonah (Jonah Chapters 1 & 2). My point is that although these people eventually were blessed, they got in the way of what God had intended. The New Testament is not any different. Here are some examples: James and John, the sons of Zebedee and Peter were supposed to be watching and praying while Christ was praying about His impending journey to the cross (Matt. 26). The Apostle Paul was no different; he, too, got in the way of what God was planning. He was spearing heading the crusades to kill the Christians (Acts 9). Even today, we are no different than these Bible greats. Be obedient to God's Word, make this year the year that you will earnestly seek His face for a change in your life in some way, shape, form or fashion.

April 4

Hope in God

Now faith is the substance of things hoped for, the evidence of things not seen. Hebrews 11:1 NLT

Many of us grew up in the church quoting this scripture…but many of us have not lived this scripture. Often times, when things go wrong in our lives, we hit the PANIC button. We go straight to, "What am I going to do now? How am I going to be able to do…?" We forget the God that we serve. I suggest to you, as Jesus did, that you already have enough faith as a believer. Once you were saved, you were given faith (John 17:6). All you have to do is activate your faith - and not sit on it. James 2:20b says, "Faith without works is dead." So, how do we activate our faith? Simple - through the spiritual disciplines of prayer, study and meditation. We have control over how much or how little we pray, study and meditate. As believers, we are to become more rooted and grounded in the Word of God, so that when life, with all of its trials, tribulations and challenges, comes our way, we will be better able to handle them. God desires us to trust His plan.

Where does your hope lie? We who have run for our very lives to God have every reason to grab the promised hope with both hands and never let go. It's an unbreakable spiritual lifeline, reaching past all appearances right to the very presence of God where Jesus, running on ahead of us, has taken up his permanent post as high priest for us, in the order of Melchizedek. Hebrews 6:19 MSG

April 5

God Is...

The Earth is the Lord's and everything in it. The world and all its people belong to him. Psalm 24:1 NLT

Sometimes, you have to minister to yourself through hymns and spiritual songs, creating a melody in your heart to the Lord (Eph. 5:19). There are going to be difficult times in your life. Sometimes, it seems as though the cycle keeps repeating itself, and you never seem to get out from underneath "it." Then, there are other times when you can move more quickly. But whatever the case may be, understand and know that God is with you, no matter what. Simply put, God Is. You may ask, what do you mean? Fill in the blank. In your life, God is......a protector, a healer, a rock, a shelter. When things are going crazy in your life, and you can't seem to make sense of it all, start singing one of your favorite songs or hymns. Focus on the words and why they minister to you so much. You will begin to notice that you stop worrying about the problem or the situation, and you begin to focus on God. Say to yourself, God is....... (name whatever it is), and you'll start to see a change in how you see that situation.

April 6

Spiritual vs. Natural Gifts

It is the one and only Spirit who distributes all these gifts.
He alone decides which gift each person should have.
1 Corinthians 12:11 NLT

Spiritual gifts versus natural gifts. From the onset, I want to encourage anyone who has not completed a spiritual gift analysis to do so. I have been a registered nurse for over 25 years and have helped hundreds of people - on the streets, in churches, in hospitals, in nursing homes and at home. I've often said that when I leave work, I don't want to do work. I often don't want to go to church or come home to work. I'M OFF DUTY! But, I can't leave it alone. It is who I am 24/7/365. No matter what happens, I will always be a nurse. That's the gift of help.

I can't help myself but to help somebody. When Christ ascended to heaven, He gave all of us spiritual gifts (1 Corinthians 12:11-12, Ephesians 4:11). These gifts are not to be boxed up with a pretty bow and placed on a shelf somewhere. They are to be used for the glory of God. So, if you have taken your spiritual gift and placed it in a box and put it on a shelf somewhere, dust it off. Take it out and put it to good use, edifying and building up the body of Christ. Use your gift for the glory of God. Don't just sit on it. God wants us to be doers of His Word and not only hearers (James 1:22).

April 7

Run Away to God

But if you remain in me and my words remain in you, you may ask for anything you want, and it will be granted! John15:7 NLT

Not long ago, I was at a retreat with my husband. It wasn't a Christian retreat workshop or anything like that. But it was a group of married couples desiring to get away from the craziness of work and family and wanting to reconnect with each other away from the constant ringing of phones and the Internet. But this had me thinking about our relationship with God. How often do we, as believers, run away to God? We know how to run away from the craziness that surrounds us. But do we really know how to run away to God? Several things or avenues come to mind. But I'll just list a few:

1. Find a space (at home, work, park, etc.) where you can be alone without interruption

2. Get up at least 30 minutes before the rest of the house to commune with God

3. Retreat at the end of the night when the house is quiet to commune with God

4. During the aforementioned times, turn off ALL electronics until your time with the Lord is done

Doing this, and much more, will give you inner peace.

April 8

Submit and Surrender

So, humble yourselves before God. Resist the devil, and he will flee from you. James 4:7 NLT

For one to submit is something that most people have a difficult time with, no matter who you are, man or woman, married or single. None of us wants to surrender or submit to anything or anyone. Many of us view it as a sign of weakness. We may view it as giving up who we are as a person. That is not the case at all. Submission in the Christian worldview is different than the worldly view. The world, often, views it as someone being in charge over your very being, telling you what to do every step of the way. But that is not how God intended for it to be. Submission has been ordained by God. Being submissive doesn't mean that you have surrendered. It doesn't mean that anybody is inferior to anybody else. God created mankind in His image, and we all have equal value. Submission is mutual between two parties. Consider submitting and surrendering yourself, your situation and your stuff for Him to manage. King Solomon says in Proverbs 16:3 (MSG) Put God in charge of your work, then what you've planned will take place.

April 9

You Are...

I will praise You, for I am fearfully and wonderfully made;
Marvelous are Your works, and that my soul knows very well.
Psalm 139:14 NLT

Not long ago, I posted a picture on social media and felt absolutely GORGEOUS. I was feeling good about myself. Confident. Excited. Then, out of nowhere, negative comments started flying from everywhere. I wasn't prepared. I didn't have my invisible shield up as I normally do. Ultimately, I failed to remember what the psalm writer declared in Psalm 139...I am fearfully and wonderfully made. I forgot that I am a child of the Most High God. Here's the thing; YOU ARE, TOO! Don't allow people to tear you down because of their own personal stuff. Don't let other people's low self-esteem bring you down. Don't let other people's negativity impact how you feel about you. You are great. You are loved. You are smart. You are intelligent. You are kind. YOU ARE BEAUTIFUL INSIDE AND OUT!

Think about what Apostle Paul says in Romans 12:17 (MSG): Don't hit back; discover beauty in everyone. If you've got it in you, get along with everybody. Don't insist on getting even; that's not for you to do. "I'll do the judging," says God. "I'll take care of it."

April 10

Unexpected Disappointments

I love the Lord because he hears my voice and my prayer for mercy. Psalm 116:1 NLT

No one said that life was going to be fair. There will always be changes in your life. The question is, how do you handle those changes? What can you do to do better? I submit to you that you begin with praise and worship to God. You see, nothing really is in our control. It's up to God. We have no control over people and circumstances; however, we have control over our prayer life and study life. How do you handle unexpected disappointments? Begin with changing your focus. Flip the situation to a positive one. Believe what God said to you. Look at the Problem Solver and not the problem. Pray for God to give you the right perspective on how to handle your situation. Talk to God more than you talk to your "neighbor." Remember: You "can do all things through Christ who strengthens you (Phil. 4:13)."

Never forget: Unrelenting disappointment leaves you heartsick, but a sudden good break can turn life around Proverbs 13:12 MSG.

Tapping into the Power Source

Jesus said to the people who believed in him, "You are truly my disciples if you remain faithful to my teaching." John 8:31 NLT

Many times, in life, we are unplugged from our Power Source. We are disconnected, detached and disengaged. It's just like at night when you fall asleep with your cellphone unplugged, and you wake up finding that you only have 20% battery life left. The same thing happens to us when we fail to study, meditate and pray; our power becomes depleted. Who is our Power Source? Jesus. He's the one that we need to stay connected to on a daily basis. John 15:4 says, in part, that we are to abide in Him as He abides in us. Verse 5 says, when we abide in Him, we bear much fruit. Without plugging into Him, we can do nothing. Nothing about our will needs to be done, but the will of the Father.

Our power source is our communication with God. Apostle Paul tells us so in Romans 8:26 (MSG) Meanwhile, the moment we get tired in the waiting, God's Spirit is right alongside helping us along. If we don't know how or what to pray, it doesn't matter. He does our praying in and for us, making prayer out of our wordless sighs, our aching groans. He knows us far better than we know ourselves, knows our pregnant condition, and keeps us present before God. That's why we can be so sure that every detail in our lives of love for God is worked into something good.

April 12

From Hurt to Halo

Confess your sins to each other and pray for each other so that you may be healed. The earnest prayer of a righteous person has great power and produces wonderful results. James 5:16 NLT

Several years ago, I had the opportunity to minister at a women's prayer breakfast. The women were of varying ages from 20s to 80s. I spoke from Mark 5:25ff regarding the woman with the issue of blood. There are many of us who are hurting deep inside. Some of us have been abused, molested, raped, discarded and left out. These are things that we keep inside. We don't share them with anyone, and as a result, those who come behind us are left behind, trying to figure out what to do next. Remember - your life is not your own. What you are going through, someone else down the line may have to go through, too, and will need a mentor or someone to talk to. I encourage you to help someone else move from hurt to halo. Someone may need a helping hand from you.

Listen to these words of encouragement: Pile your troubles on God's shoulders—he'll carry your load, he'll help you out. He'll never let good people topple into ruin. But you, God, will throw the others into a muddy bog, But the lifespan of assassins and traitors in half. And I trust in you Psalm 55:22 MSG.

April 13

Never...

The Lord is a shelter for the oppressed, a refuge in times of trouble. Psalm 9:9 NLT

You past sins don't define your destiny. The Apostle Paul tells us in Romans 3:23 that we've sinned and have fallen short of the glory of God. Our past is our past. There will always be someone who will remember who you were or what you've done in the past. Just remember - your past was never meant to be a life sentence. It was only to be a lesson to be learned. We all have had moments in our lives where we wonder where we went wrong, and we beat ourselves up continuously. It is written in Psalm 55:22 (as well as 1 Peter 5:7) that we should cast our burdens on the Lord. Whatever is trying to bring you down, turn it over to the Lord and leave it there. He's the best Person to handle your problems.

Never forget what the psalmist said in Psalm 91:5, 9-10 (NLT) Don't be afraid of the terrors of the night, nor the arrow that flies in the day. If you make the LORD your refuge, if you make the Most High your shelter, no evil will conquer you; no plague will come near your home.

April 14

Valley Experiences

My help comes from the Lord, who made heaven and Earth!
Psalm 121:2 NLT

My life and your life will never be the same. What I may have lived through you may never experience, and vice versa. But we both have faced valley experiences. Our valley experiences may be something simple or something monumental. Nevertheless, they are still valleys. God can use us in our valley experiences. How is that, you may ask? Helping us to take the focus off of us and focus on Him. Psalm 23:4 says that we will walk through the valley of the shadow of death. But it also says that God is with us. No matter how lonely it may feel while you're in your valley, just know that God is with you. The psalmist tells us in Psalm 18:20 (MSG) What a God! His road stretches straight and smooth. Every God-direction is road-tested. Everyone who runs toward him Makes it. He's guiding you along the way. Keep looking up. Stretch your hand toward God and hold on tight to His unchanging hand.

April 15

God Controls the Load in Your Valley

Don't be afraid, for I am with you. Don't be discouraged, for I am your God. I will strengthen you and help you. I will hold you up with my victorious right hand. Isaiah 41:10 NLT

Throughout life, we wear many hats. We are parents, caregivers, friends, siblings, etc. This list could go on forever. And because of the many hats we wear, we often find ourselves with highs and lows, depending on what's happening in our lives. It's in the low part of our lives where we often get caught up. That's our valley. But did you know that God actually controls the load in your valley? Often, we think that we do. But really, we don't. The only thing we have control over is our study life, prayer life and meditation life. In our valley experiences, we may feel like giving up, or maybe we feel that the world is against us. But it's in our valley experiences that God speaks to us. He promised us in Hebrews 13:5 that He would never leave us nor forsake us. Just remember while you're in your valley, that God is there with you. You're never alone. Reflect on Psalm 28:2 (MSG) I'm letting you know what I need, calling out for help and lifting my arms toward your inner sanctum.

April 16

Your Problems Have Nothing on Your Praise

Shout with joy to the Lord, all the earth! Worship the Lord with gladness. Come before him, singing with joy. Psalm 100:1-2 NLT

We all have problems. Some have problems greater than others; nevertheless, we all have problems. Many times, we have a tendency to focus on our problems more than we focus on the Problem Solver, God. Psalm 34:3 tells us that we are to magnify the Lord. Our problems aren't bigger than our praise. Our praise is what gets us through our problems. Our praise is our opportunity to focus on something and someone else other than our own problems. It's our chance to recognize that God is in control. An unknown author penned this children's song that says, "My God is so big so strong and so mighty, there's nothing my God cannot do." As you think about your day-to-day things, or when things seem to begin to overwhelm you, think about how big, strong and mighty God is compared to your problems. Magnify God, not your problems. In all that you do, remember to praise the name of God with a song, and magnify God with thanksgiving (Psalm 69:30 NKJV).

April 17

These Things

Fix your thoughts on what is true, and honorable, and right, and pure, and lovely and admirable. Think about things that are excellent and worthy of praise. Philippians 4:8 NLT

Every day, we could have a list of things we could complain about. We could complain about our mates, our children, our families, our jobs, etc. But, if we think about the things that the Apostle Paul mentions to the Philippian church, we would have a praise report. So, think about it this way: When family is getting on your nerves, think about the positives of having a family. When the job gets frustrating, think about how blessed you are to generate a paycheck. It may not be all that you want it to be, but it beats not having one at all. Thinking about the goodness of Jesus is enough to have a praiseworthy report. Every day is a day of thanksgiving. Psalm 95:2 (NKJV) encourages us to come before the presence of God with thanksgiving and to shout joyfully to Him with psalms.

Praise the Lord!

April 18

Self-Care

Those who live in the shelter of the Most High will find rest in the shadow of the Almighty. Psalm 91:1 NLT

As caregivers, we learn to take care of everyone - friends, family, foes, children, spouses, parents, grandparents, aunts and uncles. Did you see anyone missing from that list? **Yup...YOU!** You were missing from the list. When have you cared for you? When do you get the opportunity to "rest" for a while? As caregivers, we have to learn to care for ourselves. We are no good to others if we're laid up in the hospital, sick. I encourage you to take a moment to look after yourself. You're not being selfish or mean. You're looking out for your well-being so you can look after others. I get it - it's challenging to put yourself first. But you, beloved, deserve to be cared for, as well. Take a stroll in the park. Have a spa day. Have a weekend getaway with your closet friends or even by yourself. No matter what you do, or how you do it, be sure to take care of you from time to time. You deserve it, too.

April 19

God Is with You

For He Himself has said, "I will never leave you nor forsake you."
Hebrews 13:5b NKJV

Think back to when you were a kid. Do you remember a time when you were afraid or felt you were alone? Often times, for a variety of reasons, those feelings follow us through adulthood. As believers, we are reminded that God is with us wherever we go (Matthew 28:20b). Remembering that He loves us is sometimes difficult when we have a hard time loving ourselves. God's love for His children never changes. Once we are in the palm of His hand, no one can ever take us away from Him (John 10:28). As a believer in Christ, there is nothing you can do to be disowned. You now belong to the Father. You are a King's kid. You are co-heir with Christ (Gal. 4:7). That's good news! Get excited and tell someone about it. YOU'RE A KING'S KID!!

It is comforting to know that God will not forsake His people and that He takes joy in making us His people (1 Samuel 12:22). Never allow anyone to distract you from the purpose that lives within you.

April 20

It's Already Looking Better

For his anger lasts only a moment, but his favor lasts a lifetime;
weeping may last through night, but joy comes in the morning
Psalm 30:5 NLT

Oh my!!! That verse makes me want to sing, shout, dance, make a joyful noise and so much more. Listen! I can't wait for the morning. Sometimes, morning doesn't come every 24 hours in our human calculations. But one day with the Lord is like a thousand years (2 Peter 3:8).

Although things seem rough and ugly right now, it won't last forever. The pain won't last forever and the disappointment won't be there forever. There is joy on the other side of through. Just hold on to God's unchanging hand. Don't let go. Hold on tight! Joy in the morning is just around the corner. Remember -your morning can be at 7AM or 2PM. The point is that whenever God brings you through your "it," it'll be morning time. Rejoice in the Lord always (Psalms 32:11 and Philippians 4:4). God will meet you in the morning.

April 21

God Is Great

But may all of who search for you be filled with joy and gladness in you. May those who love your salvation repeatedly shout 'God is great!' Psalm 70:4 NLT

Have you chased after God lately? I mean really chased after Him? Chasing after God is your desire to be close to Him in all that you do. We are to chase after Him, morning, noon and night. It should be the first thing we do in the morning and the last thing at night. How do you do that? Through singing psalms and hymns, along with fasting and praying. Those that chase after God will be filled with joy and gladness. This is not due to a temporary situation, but a permanent reflection on your salvation. When you think about how God has kept you, you should smile. And when that happens, shout from the rooftop, "GOD IS GREAT!"

Apostle Paul gives us great words to reflect in Colossians 3:16 (MSG), Let the word of Christ dwell in you richly in all wisdom, teaching and admonishing one another in psalms and hymns and spiritual songs, singing with grace in your hearts to the Lord.

April 22

This Is the Day

This is the day the Lord has made. We will rejoice and be glad in it. Psalm 118:24 NLT

Every day we wake up is a new day. It's a day we've never seen before and one we will never see again. And because this is a great day in the Lord, we will rejoice and be glad. Why should we rejoice and be glad about it (this day)? It's rather simple. He woke you up today. You're able to read this devotional. You've had a meal (or two or three). That's something to be excited about. I get it. There are days when you just don't feel good - you ache, you hurt or someone has hurt you. It's all the more we need to lean on Jesus as your source, your provider, your protector. As we go about our day and reflect how God is with us, think about this, God's angel sets up a circle of protection around us while we pray (Psalm 34:7 MSG).

Remember - He promised that He would always be with you.

April 23

Make New Friends

Friends come and friends go, but a true friend sticks by you like family. Proverbs 18:24 MSG

As a girl scout, I learned a song that was penned by the poet Joseph Parry in 1841. The first line says, "Make new friends, but keep the old; those are silver, these are gold." However, the Girl Scouts revised it to the following: "Make new friends, but keep the old; one is silver and the other's gold." To be a great friend, one must first show themselves friendly (Ps. 18:24). It is great for you to surround yourself with great friends, but to add to your friend circle, you have to be friendly. What does that mean? One has to display love, kindness, joy and patience. But to be able to display all of that, one must embody that personally. One must extend the olive branch, even when others may not be receptive. Apostle Paul tells us in Romans 12:9 (MSG), Love from the center of who you are; don't fake it. Run for dear life from evil; hold on for dear life to good. Be good friends who love deeply; practice playing second fiddle.

Look in the mirror and declare that you are silver and gold and a great friend to many.

April 24

God Takes on Your Problems

Trust in the Lord with all your heart; do not depend on your own understanding. Seek his will in all you do, and he will show you which path to take. Proverbs 3:5-6 NLT

There will be many days that you may feel you're all alone in the world. You may feel that the world is against you and fighting you. Know that God is with you and takes on your problems. God cares for you and how you're doing. He is, after all, Abba Father. And just like our earthly father, our heavenly Father wants us to know that we don't have to take on the problems ourselves. We can and should share them with Him every chance we get. He loves us that much that He wants us to bare our souls to Him. He wants us to take everything to Him in prayer. Trust God with everything that's within you. He won't lead you astray.

God cares for you. He is concerned for you and about you. 1 Peter 5:7 tells us to give our worries, cares and concerns to God for He cares about you. Take your cares, concerns, problems and situations to the Lord in prayer and leave them there.

April 25

Self-Ministering

Don't be drunk with wine, because that will ruin your life. Instead, be filled with the Holy Spirit, singing psalms and hymns and spiritual songs among yourselves, and making music to the Lord in your hearts. Ephesians 5:18-19 NLT

Have you ever woken up in the morning with a song in your heart? Or does a particular tune come to mind when you get angry? Ephesians 5 tells us that we should be filled with the Holy Spirit singing psalms and hymns and spiritual songs. Singing unto the Lord makes Him happy. When things don't go your way, and people get on your nerves, go to God in psalm, songs and prayer. Find your favorite psalm in the Bible that speaks to you. Singing songs unto God is self-ministering. It's medicine for the soul.

When you're feeling down, shout praises to God your father. When you feel like the world is against you, worship the Lord with gladness. When things around you seem as though they are falling apart, go before God and sing with joy. Acknowledge that the Lord is God! It is He who has made us and not we ourselves (Psalm 100:3).

April 26

Run Away

Oh, that I had wings like a dove; then I would fly away and rest!
Psalm 55:6 NLT

Have you ever "run away from home?" Throughout the years, there were times I had to miss going to my home church on Sunday morning. But, as I thought about it and prayed about it, I realized that it was OK, and I wasn't going to hell just because I wasn't in church. But I began to think about how busy life can get. We run ourselves to death, doing things for everyone else and neglect time for ourselves. We put church, work, spouses and children all before ourselves. However, in order for us to take care of others, we have to take the time, moment and energy to take care of ourselves. How can we be of assistance to others if we don't know how to take care of ourselves? If we run ourselves into the ground and end up sick and in bed, what good are we to anyone else? Remember, as Jesus often stole away to have time with His Father, so should we. We should also steal away to spend time with God and with the ones that God has given to us (spouses, children, parents). It's OK to do so. Just be responsible - let the appropriate people know so that they will have an opportunity to adjust to your absence. Now, don't stay away too long…just long enough to get regenerated. GO AHEAD, GET SOME REST! BUT DON'T FORGET TO COME BACK TO REALITY!!

April 27

God's Vessel

*In a wealthy home, some utensils are made of gold and silver, and
some are made of wood and clay. The expensive utensils are used
for special occasions, and the cheap ones are for everyday use.*
2 Timothy 2:20 NLT

Do you see yourself as a vessel for God to use? Do you see yourself as a servant of the Most High God? As followers of Christ, we have a responsibility to both fellow believers and non-believers: To believers, we are to encourage and lift each other up and rebuke in love; to non-believers, we are to show them the love of Jesus. So many of us don't feel worthy to be used by God, but acceptance of self is difficult and challenging; however, it's something that needs to be practiced daily (Ps. 139:14). Emptying of self is not much easier, but being full of the Holy Spirit is essential (Romans 15:13). When God cleanses you, it is often not a pretty picture, but it is necessary (2 Corinthians 7:1). Filling of the Holy Spirit carries you, day-by-day and moment-by-moment (Proverbs 8:21). Pour out your soul in the work of the Kingdom of God (2 Timothy 2:21). Continue to do the work that God has laid out before you. It doesn't matter if you are a minister, a nurse or a teacher. We all have a responsibility to allow God to use us for His will to encourage His people.

April 28

Connecting the Dots

I cried out to the LORD, and he answered me from his holy mountain. I lay down and slept, yet I woke up in safety, for the LORD watching over me. Psalm 3:4-5 NLT

As a kid, I used to connect-the-dots, then color in the picture, of a bird, house or some other type of animal. As an adult, connecting-the-dots, apart from doing it with a child, seems…well…childish. I think about how, as a kid, I wondered what the picture would be when I was done connecting the dots - a bear, or Santa Claus or a snowman? Who knows? Sometimes that's how I feel life is like. Our day-to-day is the dots - we don't know what the final product is going to be; however, we do know who does - God. You see, only God knows what the outcome of our lives will be. It is our responsibility to connect the dots, day-by-day, by staying in the Word of God. If we become disconnected, then we become incomplete. We need the Word of God in our lives every day, not just on Sundays or on Wednesdays. Staying connected in the Word of God allows us to handle everyday life, people and circumstances. So, after you read this, turn the computer off, read one of your favorite Bible passages and get reconnected with God. Be blessed!

Don't Be Afraid

Those who live in the shelter of the Most High will find rest in the shadow of the Almighty. This I declare about the LORD: He alone is my refuge, my place of safety; he is my God, and I trust him.
Psalm 91:1-2 NLT

Psalms 91 is one of my favorites. It comforts me when I have found myself scared or frightened. It tells me that if I dwell in Him and seek refuge in Him, He will protect me. There's no need for me to be afraid of anything or anyone; God's got me! Verse 5-6 says, in part, don't be afraid of the terrors of the night or the arrows that come by day. Don't be afraid of those things that are meant to destroy at any given time. Isn't that comforting? Despite the crazy winds that were (are) happening in your life, know that God is there to comfort you. When you read further in Psalm 91, it says that God is our refuge. In the presence of the Most High, there is a soothing peace for His children. The angels in heaven are watching over you. ISN'T THAT GREAT NEWS? I'm excited that even though there may have been some destruction, chaos and confusion, MY GOD is still in control. It all remains in His hands, no matter what. Have an enjoyable day with your family and/or friends on this God-given day. Remember, although it may have RAINED last night, JESUS REIGNS FOREVER!!!!

April 30

God Knows

Yes, the LORD pours down his blessings. Our land will yield its bountiful harvest. Psalm 85:12 NLT

Sometimes, I believe God allows situations to occur just to see what our response will be. In my spiritual imagination, I can see God sitting back and looking at me (us), saying, "Are you going to trust me with the little and the big stuff? Are you going to be obedient in order to see the blessings that I have in store for you?" More often than not, we are so caught up in our current situation (or potential situation) that we fail to remember that God promised to take care of His own. Your Father in Heaven knows what you need. If He said that He will take care of you, then He will take care of you. Don't sweat the small stuff (or the big stuff, for that matter). God said that He would do it, and I believe Him - that it's, that's all!

Remember this, God's name is a place of protection—good people can run there and be safe (Proverbs 18:10 MSG).

Rejoice in knowing that God knows you and knows what's best.

May Health Awareness

American Stoke Awareness

Arthritis Awareness

Cystic Fibrosis Awareness

Hepatitis Awareness

Lupus Awareness

Nurses Week (May 6-12)

May 1

You Are Beautiful

He hath made everything beautiful in his time: also he hath set the world in their heart, so that no man can find out the work that God maketh from the beginning to the end. Ecclesiastes 3:11 KJV

Have you heard the old saying, "Beauty is in the eye of the beholder"? I believe that everything that God created is beautiful. That includes you! We often try to conform to the world's definition of beauty. If you don't remember anything else today, remember that God does all things well. He made you in His likeness and His image. You are beautiful. Start seeing yourself how God sees you. Beauty is not found in appearance. Find your beauty in how you serve, give and take care of others. As you start your day, ask God to let your beauty radiate from within. Ask Him to help you see the beauty in everything. You are beautiful! Don't let anyone tell you otherwise. Now go and have a BEAUTIFUL day.

May 2

You Are Resilient

We are troubled on every side, yet not distressed; we are perplexed, but not in despair. 2 Corinthians 4:8-9 KJV

You have the ability to recover quickly from challenges, setbacks and adversity. If you are feeling burdened or overwhelmed by life and every day situations, let me remind you that you are unstoppable. You have a job to do. Patients and families are depending on you. We understand that life is full of challenges. While we cannot control some of the challenges, we can control how we let them affect us. You can't let long shifts, poor pay and grumpy patients stop you. You've been through so much but look at you still standing, still serving and still taking care of God's people. BRAVO!!!

May 3

You Are Inspiring

Therefore encourage one another and build each other up, just as in fact you are doing. 1 Thessalonians 5:11 NIV

Most people have favor with people because of how they treat them. Showing initiative, listening to them, showing them that you care about them and giving them hope that will encourage and inspire them. Through these actions, you can inspire others to do better, fight to improve their health and strive harder to achieve the goals that they have set for themselves.

The Bible reminds us that it is God who ultimately grants favor. He can supernaturally change things. He can open doors that no man can shut. He can enable us to do what seems impossible. The Bible also reminds us that we can influence other's through our words and actions. As nurses and healthcare professionals, we must show compassion and concern, which lets people know that we truly care about them. We must listen and show a genuine interest in their problems. By doing this, we demonstrate the love of God. Today, be a good example of a person whose life has been transformed. Seek to influence and encourage others, and give them hope in these turbulent times.

Be Dedicated

I beseech you therefore, brethren, by the mercies of God, that ye present your bodies a living sacrifice, holy, acceptable unto God, which is your reasonable service. And be not conformed to this world: but be ye transformed by the renewing of your mind, that ye may prove what is that good, and acceptable, and perfect, will of God. Romans 12:1-2 KJV

How dedicated are you? Dedication is vital step for those who asked God for something specifically, worked hard to achieve it and want it to remain. I mean, who works hard to achieve something and forget about it once they've achieved it? Unless dedication is a part of your everyday life, you're going to feel like you're living only a half-life, because the purpose of life grows out of dedication. It's out of your dedication of whatever God has put into your heart and hands that you recognize why it's there and what it can be used for. As nurses, we are dedicated to caring for our patients and their families. We need to be just as dedicated to taking care of ourselves. Today, commit to doing something for yourself. And from this day forward, be dedicated to taking care of yourself like you take care of others.

May 5

Be grateful

O give thanks unto the Lord; for he is good: because his mercy endureth for ever. Psalm 118:1 KJV

Many of us live in nice homes, drive dependable cars, have food in the refrigerator and pantry and clean water. We have a lot to be grateful for. It's easy to take these blessings for granted. We must not allow a spirit of ingratitude to overtake us.

Every day we must take time to show God that we are grateful. Thank Him for your job, thank Him for your health and strength. Thank Him for your family and friends. We have so much to be grateful for. Today, decide that you are going to have an attitude of gratitude. Instead of grumbling and complaining, take a deep breath and GIVE THANKS. Remember, gratitude has medicinal purposes. It heals your mind, your body, and your spirit. Be grateful for today and never take anything for granted.

May 6

Be Encouraging

Therefore encourage one another and build each other up, just as in fact you are doing. 1 Thessalonians 5:11 NIV

There is so much going on in the world today, both positive and negative. It seems that the negative is taking over. We all need to be encouraged at some point in our lives. Being encouraging comes naturally for some but it may be hard for those who are continuously faced with challenges and disappointments in life. As nurses, we are constantly encouraging our patients. Each day purpose in your heart to send an encouraging text or email or pick up the phone and call someone to offer some encouraging words. But we must remember to encourage ourselves. An encouraging word can help someone push through a difficult situation. Whether you're looking for personal motivation, comforting a friend, reflecting on life, or trying to make a difficult decision-encouraging words can offer a new perspective. Make encouragement a part of your daily routine.

May 7

Be Trustworthy

God is not a man that he should lie; neither the son of man, that he should repents: hath he said, and shall he not do it? or hath he spoken, and shall he not make it good? Numbers 23:19 KJV

We all felt the pain of being let down by family and friends. People will disappoint you. But not our God. Our reference scripture confirms that He cannot lie. He will fulfill His promises in His own time. That is good news. While some people think they are perfect and others strive for perfection, none of us will ever be perfect. We let people down just like they let us down. The nursing profession has been voted the most trusted profession in America on many occasions. We too should be known as people who are trustworthy and dependable in our personal lives. These character traits serve as a powerful testimony in today's world and bring glory to our God.

Being a trustworthy person doesn't just happen. It takes work, commitment, dedication, and deciding to live an honest life. Here are a few things that you can do to ensure that you are living a most trusting life:

Be on time: When you say that you're going to be somewhere at a certain time, try to get there 15 minutes early.

Don't gossip: talking negatively about others behind their backs can make you look like a trouble maker.

Apologize: Apologize if you make a mistake or if you've done something wrong.

I encourage you to do something today to build trust with someone. Remember it takes time to build trusting relationships so take it one day at a time.

May 8

Be Wise

And we know that all things work together for good to them that love God, to them who are the called according to his purpose.
Romans 8:28 KJV

Making a mistake simply means that you misread, miscalculated, or misunderstood a situation or circumstance that caused you to make an error in judgement. No one – I repeat, no one – is exempt from making these types of errors! A feeling of despair should not be the result of making the mistake, but what is felt when you refuse to learn from it.

Now, what we learn depends on how we look at the results of our error in judgement. Once you have recovered from the mistake, take some time to learn from what transpired. And as you learn, hopefully, you make better choices, which can prevent you from making the same mistake again.

Today, ask God to bring you a new season of growth in you. Ask Him to allow you to gain wisdom from the mistakes you've made.

Be Optimistic

A cheerful heart is good medicine, but a broken spirit saps a person's strength Proverbs 17:22 NLT

In life, there are so many things over which we have absolutely no control. Conversely, in every situation that happens in life, there is one thing over which we have total control: our attitude. Your attitude (mindset, opinion, viewpoint) is how you think or feel about someone or something (an event or situation). Your attitude can be positive (optimistic) or negative (pessimistic).

You and only you have the power to control your attitude. After all, what happens on the inside has a way showing up on the outside, whether we want it to or not. Since it's impossible to go through life without having setbacks, challenges and adversity, choose to be optimistic, hopeful and positive. Pessimism will only guide you to a place of hopelessness. There is no positive return on engaging in negative thinking or actions. Having the right attitude can get you through just about anything. "So, a man thinketh, so is he." Today, decide to look on the bright side of things, no matter what.

May 10

Be you

I will praise thee, for I am fearfully and wonderfully made:
marvelous are thy works; and that my soul knoweth right well.
Psalm 139:14 KJV

Be the best authentic version of you. Being your true authentic self means what you say in life aligns with your actions. Over the years, I've learned that getting degrees, pursuing accolades and buying things is not nearly as important as becoming the person God created you to be. Use your time to focus on the people and things you love and to reflect and grow into the person you want to be. When we are being our own authentic self, you must surrender every part of your life to God's will every day. It also means you must surrender your own agenda to God's will. This is the only way you can become the person you were created to be. Today, decide to surrender to God. He has great things planned for you.

May 11

Be Humble

Be he giveth more grace. Wherefore he saith, God resisteth the proud, but giveth grace unto the humble. James 4:6 KJV

To be humble is to realize that you are powerless without God. It means that you can ask God for His forgiveness and trust Him for His guidance in all things. God wants us to realize and confess our complete need for Him in our lives. Humility is the opposite of pride, arrogance, and self-centeredness. True humility doesn't make you think less of yourself; it just makes you think of yourself less. It makes you willing to take a lower place than you deserve and keep quiet about things you feel strongly about. Being humble does not mean you are weak and passive. It simply means that you realize that you are helpless without God and you depend on Him for everything. Today, spend time trying to be more humble. Spend time listening to others, ask for help when you need it and ask others for their opinion and feedback from time to time.

May 12

Be Blessed

Blesses shalt thou be when thou comest in, and blessed shalt thou be when thou goest out Deuteronomy 28:6 KJV

This the day that the Lord has made, rejoice and be glad in it. We are all blessed again today with the gift of life. Sometimes we are simply too busy, distracted or overcome with grief and sadness to count our blessings. Obligations like work, family, or finances can distort our view of the blessings around us. In times like these, it is so important that we take a moment to look around and see how blessed we really are. Thank God and let's make something good happen today. Help those who need it. give to those who are less fortunate. One small positive thought in the morning and one small gesture can change your whole day. It can change someone else's whole life. Decide to be a blessing to someone today.

May 13

Be Content

Not that I speak in respect of want: for I have learned, in whatsoever state I am, therewith to be content.
Philippians 4:11 KJV

Contentment is a choice. Being content does not mean that you have settled. It means that while you are waiting on God to move on your behalf, you are very thankful and grateful for what He has already done for you. I'm not saying that you shouldn't set new goals or strive for greatness or you should simply settle for a life that doesn't bring you joy. You should set goals for yourself, dream big and work hard to attain them. Remember to enjoy the journey. Being truly content means that you know who God is and you know who you are in Him.

May 14

Be Meek

Blessed are the meek, for they shall inherit the earth.
Matthew 5:5 KJV

Most people don't truly understand what the word meek really means. The word meek means strength that is brought under control. Some people have difficulty being meek because it looks like they are weak. Being meek does not mean you're weak, it means that you are kind, strong and have self-control. What does meekness look like? Meekness is not arguing with someone when you know you are right. It means not losing your cool when your coworker is not being a team player.

Jesus is the ultimate example of meekness. He demonstrated this to us as he was going to the cross. We all know that He had the power and ability to end it all. He didn't have to ensure the brutal treatment as he traveled to Calvary. Jesus was meek for our sake. Today, be intentional about being kind and considerate to others. This includes those who are mean spirited, unapproachable and harsh. Today is going to be a good day!

May 15

Change Your Mindset

For as he thinketh in his heart, so is he. Proverbs 23:7a KJV

The mind is a powerful thing. Your mindset (attitude, outlook, approach, conviction) is an indication of what you believe and think about yourself and others. Your mindset is your own personal set of ideas, beliefs and attitudes, and can affect the way you look at life. Do you see a glass as half full or half empty? We should renew our minds daily. Acknowledge your weakness so you can learn and grow. Accept new challenges, or learn a new hobby to help you develop new skills every day. Simply put…change the way you think! Today, declare that you have the mind of Christ. Declare that it is filled with good, positive thoughts. You are well able to accomplish all that God has set before you.

Learn from Your Mistake and Move On

But the God of all grace, who have called us unto his eternal glory by Christ Jesus, after that you have suffered a while, make you perfect, stablish, strengthen, settle you. 1 Peter 5:10 KJV

Although it is extremely important to acknowledge and accept responsivity for your role in things not going as planned, it is equally important that you do not dwell on the situation. Be encouraged. Don't beat yourself up! You are not alone! God has promised that He will never leave you nor forsake you. Believe Him. Getting back on track after making a mistake will be extremely difficult if you are always down on yourself. Don't be consumed with negative thoughts and emotions. This will only severely delay your recovery process or make it next to impossible to move on. Take the initiative to get back on track. No trial, setback, disappointment, mistake, or challenge can stop His plan for your life. No matter what, each day is a gift from God and you should count it as joy!

May 17

Work as Unto the Lord

And whatsoever ye do, do it heartily, as to the Lord, and not unto men. Colossians 3:23 KJV

It is very important as a nurse that we do not get overwhelmed to the point we begin to lose focus. Understanding who you are and who's you are is very important. Therefore, your values must be reflected in all you do. Our theme scripture says, "And whatsoever ye, do, do it heartily, as to the Lord, and not unto men."

Let your light shine before men in such a way that they may see your good works, and glorify your Father who is in heaven, Matthew 5:16. If our, work as a nurse does not bring glory to God, then our work is in vain. The essence of being a nurse should not be for the money but for impact; to bring health to humanity and glory to God. This should be our focus as a nurse. So, whether you eat or drink, or whatever you don, do all to the glory of God, 1 Corinthians 10:31. Serve with good will, as to the Lord and not to men, Ephesians 6:7. God expects you to serve others, especially those in your community with good will. He wants you to use your profession as a nurse to draw men and women unto Him. In other words, let it be that when any patient encounters power of God would be manifested and they would praise God and glorify His name.

May 18

Cast Your Cares on Him

*And let the peace of Christ rule in your hearts, to which
indeed you were called in one body. And be thankful.*
Colossians 3:15 NKJV

Being a nurse in today's world can be very tasking and demanding. There is the constant work pressure of dealing with sick patients, seeing some patients die after all efforts to keep them alive fail, working long hours and not feeling appreciated. If you are married, you can add your roles of being a wife, mother, daughter, son and other personal and professional commitments to your everyday roles and responsibilities. While some of us might be use to that kind of stress, there are times it can negatively affect our body causing sickness and disease. This is why the Word of God says, "Cast all your cares on Him because He cares for you." 1 Peter 5:7.

The Spirit of God knows the danger of being anxious; the health implications and how it can affect you mentally as well. That is why He does not want you to worry or be anxious about anything. Therefore, do not be anxious about tomorrow, for tomorrow will be anxious for itself. Sufficient for the day is its trouble Matthew 6:34. You must ensure y our mind is stayed on God through His Word. Refuse to allow your heart to be troubled by the pressure you might face in your profession or in your life's endeavors.

I am sure you know that you are not immune against sickness or infections as a nurse or healthcare provider. Therefore, you must always be prayerful. Also, ensure the Word of God never departs from your heart and your lips. Like Joshua said, "This Book of the Law shall not depart from your mouth, but you shall meditate on it day and night, so that you may be careful to do according to all that is written in it. for then you will make your way prosperous, and then you will have good success" Joshua 1:8.

May 19

Ruled by Love

Love is patient, love is kind. It does not envy, it does not boast, it is not proud. It does not dishonor others, it is not self-seeking, it is not easily angered, it keeps no record of wrongs.
1 Corinthians 13:4-5, NIV

There are some nurses that have become callous as a result of the pressures we go through every day in the course of dealing with those who are sick. Most of us have seen so much sickness, disease, and death that we've become desensitized. And some hearts have become hardened and cold. Their emotions have become sore of "frozen." We must not forget the love rule…Do everything in love" 1 Corinthians 16:14.

The Word of God says, "Now hope does not disappoint, because the love of God has been poured out in our hearts by the Holy Spirit who was given to us" Romans 5:5. Can you see that? You have the love of God and not that of man in your heart. What this means is that you can perpetually display the love of God in your heart towards others. You can love others regardless of what circumstances you find them. As a nurse, one of the easiest ways to win a patient over and help them respond to treatment is to show them the love of God. Our theme verse says, "Love is patient, love is kind, does not dishonor others, it is not easily angered." If you are patient, kind, do not dishonor and do not easily get angered by your patients or your colleagues, that is the love of God being demonstrated by you.

As a nurse, my prayer and desire for you is that the Lord directs your hearts into God's love and Christ's perseverance. This way you would find it very easy to love anyone, especially your patients and colleagues.

May 20

God's Outstretched Hand of Healing

And by the hands of the apostles were many signs and wonders wrought among the people. Acts 5:12a KJV

As Christian nurse, understand that you are God outstretched hands of healing to your world. In other words, you are nurse with a difference. You God's healing agent as you care for your patients. When a patient encounters you, it should feel like they have encountered an angel sent by God. When you touch a patient, it should be a touch of healing. Remember, the Word of God says, "They shall lay hands on the sick, and they shall recover" Mark 16:18b. Your words should be words of hope, reassurance, faith and healing.

Let it be that through your hands, healing and health are restored to the patients that you care for. Our theme scripture shows us how it happened with the apostles. And by the hands of the apostles were many signs and wonders wrought among the people. If the apostles could perform healing and other miracles, you can too.

Remember, you are God's healing hands on this earth. And these signs will follow those who believe: In My name they will cast out demons; they will speak with new tongues; they will take up serpents; and if they drink anything deadly, it will by no means hurt them; they will lay hands on the sick, and they will recover Mark 16:17-18. This is how the Spirit of God sees you. He wants you to be God's outstretch hands to your patients and every other person that you encounter.

May 21

God's Masterpiece

For we are God's masterpiece. He has created us anew in Christ
Jesus, so we can do the good things he planned for us long ago.
Ephesians 2:10 NLT

Our theme verse is very clear. It says YOU are God's workmanship, created in Christ Jesus to do good works, which God destined you to do in life. Isn't that amazing? You are God's work and you were created to do good. WOW! The nursing profession is known to be the most trusted of all professions. Not only are we trusted, we are respectful, hardworking, caring, compassionate, kind and disciplined. Become an example for other nurses. Remember you are God's workmanship, His handiwork. Show forth the goodness of God as you are caring for your patients, use your healing hands, your soothing voice and your infectious spirit to bring glory to His name. Not to us, O Lord, not to us, but to your name give glory, for the sake of your steadfast love and your faithfulness! Psalm 115:1

When You Don't Know What to Say

For the Holy Ghost shall teach you in the same hour what ye
ought to say. Luke 12:12 KJV

There are times that we don't have the words to comfort our patients and their family members. Some situations leave us speechless. Have you ever had to hold a patient's hand while the doctor told them that there was nothing, they could do to help them get better? Have you had to stand at the bedside with the family as the doctor told them their loved one had no brain activity? These are very difficult times for the family and those healthcare providers taking care of the patient.

Based on Luke 12:12, we can be reassured that the Holy Spirit with teach us what to say. The promise is that the Holy Spirit will help you in any setting and frightening situations. One of the reasons I really want you to enjoy and meditate on this particular scripture is that I have found it to be true and amazing in my own professional practice as well as my personal life. There have been times in my 20+ years of practice that I have asked the Holy Spirit to fill my mouth with comforting words for my patients and their family members.

Today, I want you to focus on letting the Holy Spirit be your helper, teacher and guide. Have confidence that God will speak to you through the Holy Spirit. Now is the time to step out on faith, put aside all fear, and trust in the Holy Spirit to teach you what to say to your patients today.

Do Not Grow Weary

And let us not be weary in well doing: for in due season we shall reap, if we faith not. Galatians 6:9 KJV

Nursing is an extremely stressful profession. From nursing school to the retirement party, we are challenged on a daily basis with a variety of stressors as we care for our patients. These job-related stresses can take a toll on the mind, body and spirit of these professionals. This stress can affect the quality of patient care and outcomes. Work-related stress may also impact job satisfaction, workforce stability, and safety in the healthcare environment. Somedays seem more stressful than others. The stress that we face every day can lead to burnout. Burnout is a special type of job stress. it is a state of physical, emotional or mental exhaustion combined with doubts about competence and decreased value of one's work.

Here are few strategies to help you prevent, reduce, address and recover from burnout:

Take a break (stop selling your vacation days and working your off days)

Acknowledge your limitations (I can no longer work 12-hour shifts or care for 7-10 patients)

Consider a job change (look for a position that's less demanding)

Take care of yourself (eat a well-balanced diet, drink plenty of water, lose weight if you need too and get enough sleep)

Nurses often care for everyone else but forget about themselves. This has to change. Today, I want you to ask the Lord to walk beside you and help you to not grow weary. Ask God to give you the fruits of the spirit: love, joy, peace, patience, gentleness, goodness, faithfulness, meekness, and self-control (Galatians 5:22-23. Also ask Him to help you make a difference in the lives of every person you encounter today. What an amazing day this will be!

May 24

Have Faith

But without faith it is impossible to please Him: for he that comes to God must believer that He is and that He is a rewarder of them that diligently seek Him. Hebrews 11:6 KJV

We must have faith. It pleases God. We stand on faith; we live by faith. The Bible teaches that faith is the only approach that we have to God. Nurses live out their faith every day as they provide physical, emotional, and spiritual care to their patients. What is faith? It is the confidence or trust in something or someone. How do you get faith? Growing in faith requires one to believer in God and maintain a close and personal relationship with Him. When you build a relationship with a person, you spend time with them, you talk to them, and you share your deep thoughts and personal ideas with them. Building a relationship with God is no different. You spent time with Him through prayer, bible study and worship.

If it is impossible to please God without faith. The opposite is also true; faith is what please God. Faith is important to Jesus, He responded to it everywhere He went. So, we can come to a conclusion that God responds to our faith. It please Him, it moves Him to act and it is essential in the life of the believer. Today, I want to have faith in God. He can move those mountains. He can open those closed doors. He can heal the sick. Just have faith and stand on His word.

May 25

Your New Identity-

Therefore if any man be in Christ, he is a new creature: old things are passed away; behold all things are become new.
2 Corinthians 5:17 KJV

You are very special to God regardless of your past. Your past and the wrongs you've done are of no significance to your new identity. The Word of God says, "Therefore if any man be in Christ, he is a new creature: old things are passed away; behold all things are become new" 2 Corinthians 5:17. The Lord Jesus took care of those things you are holding on to or that are keeping you from fully enjoying your life. He died so that we could have life and have it more abundantly.

Unlike people, God doesn't keep records of all the bad things you've done. He gave you a completely new identity in Him. But you are a chose generation, a royal priesthood, a holy nation, His own special people, that you may proclaim the praises of Him who called you out of darkness into His marvelous light, 1 Peter 2:9. This is how God sees: a chosen generation, a royal priesthood, a holy nation, and His own special people. So, refuse to allow anyone tell you or make you feel otherwise. And please be careful with the words you say about yourself. Speak positive things about yourself and others.

Regardless of the circumstances of your birth, background, location or qualifications, what really count is who and what the Lord has made you. He values you so much that He gave His Son's life for you. He brought you out of the deep dark place and placed you on a hill to stay. He brought me up also out of a horrible pit, out of the miry clay, and set my feet upon a rock, and established my goings Psalm 40:2. This is your identity. So, embrace it and be happy.

May 26

The Wisdom of God

If any of you lack wisdom, let him as of God, who gives to all liberally and without reproach, and it will be given to him.
James 1:5 NKJV

Where does your wisdom come from? Who or what do you turn to in your time of need, when you are stressed or when you have an important decision to make?

Whenever I find myself not understanding a situation, I pray for wisdom. I believe that if I asked the Lord for wisdom to understand a situation that He would answer. It's imperative that we make it a habit to always seek the Lord and His word first when we need wisdom or advice regarding anything. God will order your footsteps if you let Him. Ask God to give you understanding, knowledge and wisdom in every situation. Ask Him to help you learn how to be more understanding, patient and compassionate towards others.

As nurses we develop wisdom through practice. Wisdom comes from caring for countless patients over time. God will give you insight into important issues but you have to ask for it. ask God to give you insight on how to care for your patient. Ask Him to show you what's going on with your patient. Today, take a few minutes to ask God to give you wisdom in every situation that you may face. Ask Him to give you wisdom in difficulty situations while taking care of your patients. Remember to ask.

May 27

I'm An Overcomer

For whatsoever is born of God overcometh the world: and
this is the victory that overcometh the world, even our faith.
1 John 5:4 KJV

Have you been through one different season after another? Maybe you've been sick for a long time and it doesn't like you're going to get well. Or perhaps you've lost your job or your home. Whatever you've faced, you are not alone. Every born-again person has the capacity to overcome the world. But overcoming difficult situations seem impossible when you're going through them. Be encouraged! We must understand that life is not void of trials and tribulations. Your attitude towards these challenges matters. Remember our brother Job? He lost everything; his wealth, authority, family, cattle, health, and friendships (Job 1:13-22). But he never gave up or cursed God. He overcame.

The Word of God is filled with accounts of people who endured trials and tribulations, pain, suffering, hardship, and loss. But if you do a little research, you will see that they persevered because they knew that nothing—nothing even death—could separate them from God's love and promises.

The Word of God says So do not worry, saying, 'What shall we eat?' or 'What shall we drink?' or 'What shall we wear? For the Gentiles strive after all these things, and your heavenly Father knows that you need them.' Can you see that? Decide today not ever allow yourself to be subjected to stressful conditions. Scripture reminds us, "Commit everything you do to the LORD. Trust him, and he will help you," Psalm 37:5. Talk to God, pray in the Spirit often and meditate on God's Word day and night.

May 28

God Is Bigger Than Any Problem

Don't' be afraid, for I am with you. Don't be discouraged, for I am you're your God. I will strengthen you and help you. I will hold you up with my victorious right hand. Isaiah 41:10 NLT

The world is in great turmoil right now. Things are happening in the world today that is causing the hearts of people to become hard and filled with despair. Many are in fear of contracting disease, losing their jobs and subsequently their homes and cars. People are perplexed, feeling helpless and hopeless. But BELIEVERS should not be feeling perplexed, helpless or hopeless. Why? Because we stand on the Word of God. We already know that the things that are happening in the world would happen. There will be great earthquakes, and in many places, people will starve to death and suffer terrible diseases. All sort of frightening things will be seen in the sky, Luke 21:11. Do not be afraid. And do not allow your faith in the Lord to be shaken because He is with you.

I tell my colleagues every day, refuse to fear but be cautious. Use universal precautions and wear all of the personal protective equipment that is offered to you. I also tell them to remember to pray over themselves and their colleagues. "There shall no evil befall thee, neither shall any plague come nigh thy dwelling. For he shall give his angels charge over thee, to keep thee in thy ways" Psalm 91:10-11. We have to keep each other covered in these uncertain times. Spend time in prayer rather than spending your precious time worrying or watching the news which will create fear in your heart.

Create time to study the Word of God. As you study, also pray for God's protection and guidance for you, your loved ones and your colleagues. You should not be among those spreading the fear, rather, spread the messages of hope to encourage the faith of others. Remember, God is NOT sleep. He is aware of EVERTYING that is going on.

Keep Your Faith in These Difficulty Times

They strengthened the believers. They encouraged them to continue in the faith reminding them that we must suffer many hardships to enter the Kingdom of God, and encouraged them to remain true to the faith. We must pass through many troubles to enter the Kingdom of God, they taught. Acts 14:22 NLT

Maintaining your faith in times of trials, troubles tribulations, persecutions, problem or whatever challenges you might face is very important. Faith is the decision to press, no matter the circumstances. And the more you choose to press through difficult situations, the greater your faith will grow. The Word of God asks, "Who shall separate us from the love of Christ? Shall trouble or hardship or persecution or famine or nakedness or danger or sword?" Romans 8:35. It is of no use denying the fact that these are difficult times. But nothing can separate us from God. Only the Word of God can stabilize you and build your faith. Hear what the Lord said, "I have told you these things, so that in me you may have peace. In this world you will have trouble. But take heart! I have overcome the world" John 16:33. The Lord lets us know that there would always be tribulations in this life, but He reminds us to be strong because He has overcome the world just for you.

One sure way you can keep your faith in these difficult times is to study the Word of God more. Remember the Word of God says, "So then faith comes by hearing, and hearing by the word of God," Romans 10:17. Today, remember to read the Word of God to strengthen your faith.

May 30

Love Like Christ

This is my commandment, that ye love one another, as I have loved you. John 15:12 KJV

What is love? Love is not a feeling. There are several kinds of love:

Eros is romantic love between a man and a woman

Phileo is the brotherly love we feel for friends and companions

Storage is the love family members have for each other

Agape is God's love—the love He extends to everyone

Loving like Jesus is the best way to love. When we love like Him, we can clearly see the needs of those around us. Jesus' model of love is perfect. If we truly want to love like Jesus, we have to open our hears and our minds. We have to be vulnerable and ready to love unconditionally.

I honestly think that all of us want to love like Jesus. Who doesn't want to be generous, forgiving, and compassionate enough to love unconditionally? Some people actually try to love unconditionally but because of hurt betrayal and injustice, flesh gets in the way. God command is to love in the agape way of loving. Agape love results in action, not feelings. Agape love is a choice. Agape love is the love the world needs. Today, ask the Lord to help you to love like Him.

May 31

It's Okay to Cry

Jesus wept. John 11:35

Jesus cried? Yes, He did. The importance of Jesus wept is recorded in the Gospel of John. Jesus shows us that sorrow and grief is something that we will experience. I think that when we read the Bible, we tend to forget that Jesus had a human side. It can be easy to forget that Jesus as a higher being could feel emotions. Remember when Jesus cried over his friend Lazarus? He knew that he could and would raise him from the dead but, He still cried. We cry when we lose a loved one even though we know that they knew the Lord and weren't suffering anymore.

Death is a devastating reality of humanity. We know that death is inevitable but it does not make it any easier to experience. It's especially hard to swallow when death comes unexpectedly or tragically. Working in healthcare can be emotionally draining. Nurses are human, not robots. Having and embracing this humanity in our roles is crucial in providing patient-centered care. It also allows our genuine empathy, compassion, and kindness to be shown to our patient's when it matters the most. As nurses, we are on the frontline where we see more death in a week's time than some people might see over a lifetime. It's a lot. It's okay to cry with and for your patients. Crying is a natural response. It's okay to cry. In fact, crying has many health benefits. It regulates emotions, reduces distress, calms and soothes, and releases oxytocin and endorphins. Crying can be therapeutic. If you feel the need to release a tear or two for your family, friends or your patients it's okay. After all Jesus wept. "Weeping may tarry for the night, but joy comes with the morning," Psalm 30:5. "And when that morning comes, death shall be no more, neither shall there be mourning, nor crying, nor pain anymore," Revelation 21:4.

June Health Awareness

Alzheimer's Awareness

Men's Health Month

National Scleroderma Awareness

Scoliosis Awareness

June 1

Why Worry When You Can Pray

Then Jesus said come to me all of you who are weary and carry heavy burdens, and I will give you rest. Take my yoke upon you; let me teach you because I am humble and gentle at heart, and you will find rest for your souls. For my yoke is easy to bear, and the burden I give you is light. Matthew 11:28-30 NLT

Nurses worry so much for those they provide care that they often forget to take time out for themselves. The daily stress of meeting the needs of others can become overwhelming, but God tells us to take everything to Him in prayer. We can rest on the promises of God, knowing that there is nothing that we go through or experience in this life that we have to face alone. I encourage you to keep on praying today. Seek God and trust that He will turn your worry into inexplicable peace. Worry weighs a person down; an encouraging word cheers a person up (Proverbs 12:25).

Healing A Wounded Heart

He heals the broken-hearted and bandages their wounds.
Psalm 147:3 NLT

When we think of all the conditions of the heart in the natural realm, including hypertension, coronary heart disease, cardiovascular disorders, and cardiac arrest, they all cause heart damage. If we take a look at matters of the heart in the spiritual realm, they also cause damage as well. When we hold on to past hurt, envy, jealousy, and many other things, we damage our hearts, but there is good news! God can heal us from all of these things.

Think about a time when you encountered a bitter or angry co-worker. Did you take time to reflect on what the real issue could be? Even take a moment and reflect on a situation or circumstances that have caused your heart to become damaged or broken. You may be holding on to something someone did or said to you, but don't let it take root in your heart. Allow God to make you whole again. Ask Him to restore your heart into a place of love.

June 3

Watch Your Words, Watch Your Thoughts

And do not be conformed to this world, but be transformed by the renewing of your mind, that you may prove what is that good and acceptable and perfect will of God. Romans 12:2 NKJV

Once we speak, try as we may, we will never be able to take back our words. One analogy that comes to mind is attempting to get toothpaste back into the tube after squeezing it onto a brush. Good luck with that-it's impossible. The word of God in Luke 6:45 says, "for out of the abundance of the heart the mouth speaks." We must be careful to watch our words and our thoughts. We must seek God for wisdom in every situation. Asking God to help us listen from our hearts and to develop the ability to discern the struggles of others is necessary for our daily lives. We must continually seek God in our thoughts and through prayer.

God Will Take Care of You

The Lord is my shepherd; I lack nothing. He makes me lie down in green pastures; he leads me beside quiet waters, he refreshes my soul. Even though I walk through the darkest valley, I will fear no evil, for you are with me; your rod and your staff, they comfort me. Surely your goodness and love will follow me all the days of my life, and I will dwell in the house of the Lord forever. Psalm 23:1-4, 6 NIV

God reminds us in Philippians 4:19 that He will supply all of our needs according to His riches in glory. I am sure there were times in each of our lives when we wondered if God heard our prayers. Even now as we try to navigate the uncertainty of our time, we may have that question in our hearts. I want to assure you that God hears and answers all that we ask according to His will. His will may not align with our will in the moment but we are guaranteed that all things will work together for good if we continue to abide in His Will.

Even in those moments when we doubt God, He is still right there. God knows far better what we need than we do. God provides us with daily strength to care for others. He gives us the ability to meet their physical, spiritual, psychosocial, and mental needs. How much more will He do for those He loves? How much more will He do for you?

June 5

God is Simply Amazing

Understand, therefore, that the Lord your God is indeed God. He is the faithful God who keeps his covenant for a thousand generations and lavishes his unfailing love on those who love him and obey his commands. Deuteronomy 7:9 NLT

Through every trial, struggle, and season of life, God has been the solid rock. I realize now that nothing that happens in this life, no matter how shocking it might be to us, can take God by surprise. He sees the end from the beginning and is the author and finisher of our faith. God makes no mistakes, and He takes care of His own. Even in those times when we may want to give up, God reminds us that He is concerned about the things that concern us. Even when we cannot depend on others, God always comes through for us. We should always be thankful for this blessing. He is the creator of the universe, and the sovereign Lord over all, yet when we call out to Him, he hears us. God continues to bless us better than we behave. God is worthy of praise forever and always!

June 6

Be Kind to Others

And the King will say, I tell you the truth when you did it to one of the least of these my brothers and sisters, you were doing it to me!" Matthew 25:40 NLT

Words can both kill and give life. They are either poison or fruit. You can choose to be kind to others, or you can choose to act otherwise. Either way, the choice rests with you. Proverbs 18:21 declares that "death and life are in the power of the tongue, And those who love it will eat its fruit."

As believers, we must be careful of the words we speak. There are many hurting people in this world. The love of Christ should shine so brightly in us and through us that when they have a simple encounter with us, they also have an encounter with the heart of God. A simple smile can change a person's entire day. A kind word could change their whole outlook on life. We can never know what someone else has to endure daily, so every day, make it your aim to be a light in the darkness.

Ask the Lord to help you be the person that you would need were you in their situation. God desires for us to treat others as we want to be treated.

Keep the Faith

And let us not grow weary while doing good, for in due season we shall reap if we do not lose heart. Galatians 6:9 NKJV

Have you ever asked God to reveal the things you needed to see to move into the next phase of your life? Have you ever felt like God just doesn't understand your needs? Have you ever felt like giving up hope and slowly give in to your feelings of despair? How about wanting to give up on a dream, vision, or passion because your life seems stuck in just one place? As a believer, you know in theory that God is more than able to do what He said, but nothing is happening for you.

What do you do? Do you give up? Do you feed yourself false reasons for why things will never work in your favor? Or do you turn to the source of your hope and strength?

How do you hold fast and keep the faith when the enemy of faith, which is doubt, continues to haunt you?

Well, I have been guilty of all of this. God spoke to me amid these feelings and said, "Trust Me, I know far better than you. I can see way ahead, and I know what lies before you. I'm protecting you; I'm preparing you; I'm working some things out in you and for you. Don't look at others, but keep your focus on me. I will do just what I said I would do. Trust and believe that He is doing the same for you even now. So, if any of you have felt like I do, God wants me to tell you that your end will be greater than your beginning, and even when you don't understand, keep believing that He knows best.

June 8

You Are on God's Mind

For God so loved the world that He gave His only begotten Son,
that whoever believes in Him should not perish but have
everlasting life. John 3:16 NKJV

By general consensus, I think it is fair to say that we sometimes find ourselves wondering if God is really concerned about us. We may look at the success of "the wicked," those who don't give God the time of day and compare it to our lives and wonder why they are being rewarded for "bad behavior."

During our everyday lives, we think about how we care for the sick and take on the needs of others, including patients, families, and loved ones, with no reward. God reminds us in Isaiah 26:3 that He will keep in perfect peace all who trust in him and all whose minds are fixed on him. God wants to tell us that we are always on his mind and that he is concerned about every area of our lives. Like the good Father that He is, God watches over His children. God cares for us so much that He gave his only son for the sins of this world. He sacrificed for us more than we can ever deserve because of the depth of his love for us.

June 9

Packed for the Journey

The Lord himself goes before you and will be with you; he will never leave you nor forsake you. Do not be afraid; do not be discouraged. Deuteronomy 31:8 NIV

As I was driving and thinking about all the things, I needed to do to prepare for my road trip, God spoke to me. I thought about how I needed to wake the kids at 3:30am so we could get on the road while it's dark and there was less traffic. I thought about how I would pack their blankets so I could cover them in the car and allow them to sleep comfortably. I thought about all the things I needed to pack for them. As a parent, I thought to myself (not for the first-time mind you,) "they have the easy job."

At that moment, God spoke to me, saying, "this is what I do for you, my child."

In those dark moments of your life, I wrap you in my loving arms and allow you to rest. God says, "I have already gone before you and "packed" all the things that you need for this journey called life." God wants us to know that we are packed for the trip. He has already gone before us and prepared the way. This journey called life can seem hard, but God has equipped us with all that we need.

June 10

Stay Focused

Lord, if it's you," Peter replied, "tell me to come to you on the water." "Come," he said. Then, Peter got down out of the boat, walked on water and came toward Jesus. But when he saw the wind, he was afraid and, beginning to sink, cried out, "Lord, save me!" Immediately Jesus reached out his hand and caught him. "You of little faith," he said, "why did you doubt?"
Matthew 14:28-31 NIV

My encouragement for you today is simply this: don't lose focus. Today I was walking to lunch, and I was so focused on my phone that I stepped onto the wrong path. By the time I realized it, I was far past where I should have been. I missed the opportunity to take the most convenient route to get to my destination. Despite missing the mark, I kept walking to my destination; just on a longer path God reminded me that sometimes we are so focused on the things around us that we miss what He has for us. We are so caught up in the many responsibilities that we have and the many tasks we have to juggle that we forget to take a moment to simply be still in His presence. The good news is that even though I missed my target, I was redirected. I was delayed, but I was not denied entry or access.

It sometimes takes longer to get where we want to go in life because we are not paying attention the first time around. God wants us to stay focused on Him so that we don't miss what He is doing the first time but if we do, God in His mercy is willing to redirect us and still grant us access to Him. The story of Peter walking on water in Matthew is evidence of the consequence of becoming distracted. While Peter's heart and eyes were fixed on Jesus, he was able to do the impossible. Peter allowed his fear to distract him from God's supernatural power in the same way that we allow things to distract us from who God is and what He can do in our life. When Peter cried out to Jesus, He did not allow Peter to drown. Instead, Jesus reached out to Peter and rescued him not just from the waves but from himself. This same Lord is offering to rescue us from our many burdens and to give us rest and peace in His presence.

June 11

Better Days Ahead

The future glory of this temple will be greater than its past glory, says the Lord of heaven's armies. And in this place I will bring peace. I, the Lord of heaven's armies have spoken. Haggai 2:9 NLT

If we aren't careful, we could lose ourselves in the doom, gloom and despair of the world around us. It almost seems like it would be much easier to stop trying to hold it together so tightly and simply let ourselves go. It would be easy to wallow in self-pity, despair, distress and fear but it would not be in line with scripture.

The children of the Lord are not called to live and weep as though they have no hope when our hope is rooted in the Lord. We know that despite everything happening around us, and despite things seeming as if they will never end, there will be better days.

We know this, and we believe it because God said so, there is no simpler explanation and no better reason to believe anything.

Read your bible. You will find the many times believers are warned of the darkness and devastation that was "to come" and that we are currently experiencing in our time. There is no record of God simply packing up His things after delivering the bad news and riding off in the opposite direction. Instead, what we get are assurances that no matter how rocky things get, we will never be alone. We can take comfort in knowing that better days are awaiting us up ahead.

Growing in Faith

My brethren, count it all joy when ye fall into divers temptations; knowing this, that the trying of your faith worketh patience James 1:2-3 NKJV

There are many challenges that we each encounter during different seasons of our lives. I trust and accept that each season is an opportunity to grow my faith. Each experience in life is a building block for the future. That means that during those challenging times in life, we are to learn something about ourselves and God. God desires to see growth in each of us, especially in the area of our faith. God has shown up for us in so many ways, too numerous to count. Growing in faith requires us to study God's word, spend time in prayer, and worship him for who he is in our lives. My definition of faith would be trusting God to do what I'm unable to do in my own strength, but the Bible's definition is even better. Faith is the building block of hope. Faith is the substance that goes into bringing to life the things that we cannot see in the physical, but that we ask God for in the Spirit. Faith is the reliance on God's faithfulness to exact His will in our lives, and it is strengthened in adversity. Difficult situations put us in a position to trust God, and the more we believe him, the stronger we become.

June 13

God's Perfect Plan

For I know the plans I have for you, says the Lord. They are plans for good and not for disaster, to give you a future and a hope.
Jeremiah 29:11 NLT

God has a plan for each of our lives. His word tells us in Jeremiah 1:5, that He knew us in our mother's womb and that He set us apart. Have you ever asked yourself, "What is it that God desires for me?" Have you ever questioned why you had to experience difficulties just to learn a lesson? Have you ever found yourself asking, "Why me, Lord?"

If you are like most people, you would answer yes to at least one of these questions. There are moments in each of our lives when we wonder what is going on, but what I have found is that each season of our life prepares us for what is to come. God knew that you would become a nurse, a lawyer, a doctor, or whichever profession you have chosen. God already knew, and He prepared you for the journey. Often times, we focus on our situations more than God's plan for our life, but God is a perfect God, and His plans for our lives are complete. God knows what it will take for each of us to fulfill His will in our life. I challenge you today to totally trust God and His perfect plans. His ways are higher than our ways, and his plans will exceed anything we can ever imagine.

Favor with The King

Go and gather together all the Jews of Susa and fast for me. Do not eat and drink for three days, night or day. My maids and will do the same. And then, though it is against the law, I will go in to see the king. If I must die. I must die. Esther 4:16 NLT

Esther is a familiar character from the Old Testament. She was a brave young woman who gave endlessly of herself. Esther placed the needs of others above her own and was highly favored by God. Esther's life reminds us that God will grant you favor with Him, but that he will also grant you favor with men. Esther found favor with the king, and as a result, saved so many lives, including her own. Esther possessed many qualities, including her ability to problem-solve. Esther was a thinker and mentally quick in her approach to communicating with others. Esther was a wise woman who knew when to keep quiet, especially when dealing with authority. Esther was courageous, risking her life for the sake of others. Although Esther was in a position of power and wealth, she realized that she needed God's direction and wisdom. Esther understood the importance of fasting and praying, which encourages believers to take the same approach when faced with difficult situations.

June 15

Faith

Now faith is the substance of things hoped for, the evidence of things not seen. Hebrews 11:1 NKJV

There are circumstances that we each face, whether it be health challenges, financial difficulties, marital issues, employment challenges, or moments of weakness in our spiritual walk with God. No matter what the problem may be, we must trust God and remember that He has worked things out in our favor. I heard someone say that a faith that can't be tested can't be trusted, and I believe that. There's a difference between hearing about what God can do and witnessing it in our own lives. I can say in faith that I know God is a healer, but when God heals me, it elevates my faith. God uses life experience to build our faith. The question remains do you trust him. Sometimes we have to be honest with God and ourselves and ask God to help our unbelief.

The Gift of An Open Door

Every good gift and every perfect gift is from above and comes down from the Father of lights, with whom there is no variation or shadow of turning. James 1:17 NKJV

Every day that we open our eyes and take our first conscious breath is a gift from God. A gift is something that we don't have to pay for but is freely given if we choose to accept it. God wants to do so many things in our lives. When we look at the blessings pronounced in Deuteronomy over the lives of a faith-filled believer, it becomes abundantly clear that God desires us to prosper in every area of our lives. Sometimes we are so busy focusing on the closed doors and missed opportunities that we don't recognize how many doors God has opened for us. He continually provides all that we need. He never changes or casts a shifting shadow. I challenge you today to meditate on all the gifts and open doors that God has given you.

June 17

God's Assignment

I am the vine; you are the branches. He who abides in Me, and I
in him, bears much fruit; for without Me, you can do nothing.
John 15:5 NKJV

If we do what God instructs us to do, we will be in the center of His will. How difficult is it to do what God tells you to do? If we're sincere in our answer, we may confess that our obedience to God is sometimes linked to our emotions and limited foresight.

Do you trust God to lead you in every area of your life? Do you follow God even when you cannot see what His end-goal is? God has an assignment for each of us. Often, we are unclear on the next steps that we should take or the ideas that we should pursue because we have not taken the time to listen clearly to Him and follow his direction. God's word reminds us that apart from Him, we can do nothing. John 15:5. To complete our God-given assignments, we must place Him at the center of all we say and do.

June 18

God's Direction

Thy word is a lamp unto my feet and a light unto my path.
Psalm 119:105 KJV

We can't trust our feelings and experiences to be an effective way of understanding God. We should always filter our experiences through the word of God. If we don't study God's word, our understanding may become distorted, and we may find ourselves traveling in the wrong direction. We have become heavily reliant on GPS and navigation systems to help us in our daily commute. This man-made source of direction has an impressive track-record of accuracy, but of course, it is flawed and sometimes makes mistakes. Sometimes, the system itself is not in error, but because we are in control, the information provided is a reflection of our own incorrect input.

God's directions, however, are one hundred percent perfect all the time. He is sovereign, omnipotent, and, most of all, not dependent on us for anything. We can trust God's direction to lead us to the right path. God's word is a lamp unto our feet and a light unto our path. He leads us according to the Holy Spirit. The word of God is our roadmap in life, and we would be lost without it. In Matthew 4:18-20, Jesus told Simon-Peter, and his brother Andrew to follow him. He later told James, John, and their father Zebedee to follow him also. They were all obedient to God's direction. Although God may provide more details in somethings and less in others, we must be willing to trust the direction in which he is leading us.

June 19

Obey God

Now it shall come to pass, if you diligently obey the voice of the Lord your God, to observe carefully all His commandments which I command you today, that the Lord your God will set you high above all nations of the earth. Deuteronomy 28:1 NKJV

God will reveal what he has for us to do, and we must be willing to obey. As Moses obeyed God, he accomplished what he could not do in his own strength. Because of his relationship and walk with God, Moses, towards the end of His life, was able to give one final speech to the children of Israel, reminding them of the depth of God's love for them. He spoke about the many miracles God performed for them, and the many times he spared them from certain destruction. He presented them with options and encouraged them to obey God so that the days of their lives could be extended. God used Moses to reveal His purpose in the lives of the Israelites. The same is true for us today. God will reveal His purpose and always confirm his word.

Sometimes we need to be reminded of how important it is to be obedient to God. In the same way that obedience deepened the connection between God and Moses, it will do the same thing for us.

We must rely totally on God at all times. When we recognize and accept that we can do nothing in our own strength, it changes everything.

June 20

Divine Connections

Though one may be overpowered by another, two can withstand him. And a threefold cord is not quickly broken.
Ecclesiastes 4:12 NKJV

God will send the right people into our life at the right moments. There are those who God has ordained to be in our lives. Romans 8:29 says, "For from the very beginning God decided those who came to him and all along he knew who would, should become like his son so that his son would be the first with many brothers." So, God knows us and predestined us in the image of Jesus. Jesus is a divine connection in our lives. When God connects you with others, it is all a part of your divine assignment. People are assigned to your life for different reasons and seasons. Stay connected unless you hear differently from God. There is something he desires to do in you or in the other person.

June 21

Let Me Fight for You

My grace is all you need. My power works best in weakness, so now I am glad to boast about my weaknesses so that the power of Christ can work through me. 2 Corinthians 12:9 NLT

There are some battles that we can't fight on our own. We need the power of God to move in every situation, but some are so overwhelming that all we can do is run to Him. During our busy workdays and while caring for others, we face many challenges. It may be a co-worker, a demanding boss, unsaved friends or family who come against us for whatever reason. We must remember that spiritual fights require us to be cloaked in the whole armor of God. We don't have the physical strength to fight some of the battles we encounter daily. We are reminded in the word that reminds us that some battles will not be won in our own strength but through God's power.

June 22

Have Faith in God

Have faith in God, Jesus answered. Truly I tell you, if anyone says to this mountain, 'Go throw yourself into the sea,' and does not doubt in their heart but believes that what they say will happen, it will be done for them. Therefore I tell you, whatever you ask for in prayer, believe that you have received it, and it will be yours. Mark 11:22-24 NIV

God will allow things to happen in our lives to test our faith. A faith lesson is not the time to doubt all that God has promised. Doubt often arises in times of struggle. Maybe we didn't get a new job, a new house or a new car we desired. Perhaps we lost a loved one or didn't receive the doctor's report we anticipated. God is faithful, and just, therefore, we must trust Him. We can have anything that we ask in the name of Jesus according to his perfect and pleasing will. We must have faith in God and exactly trust what he says.

June 23

A Friend Like None Other

Greater love has no one than this than to lay down one's life for his friends. John 15:13 NIV

What is a friend? A friend is defined as a person you know, like, and trust. What is a ride or die, friend? A ride or die friend is someone who loves you and is willing to do anything for you. What is a day one? A day one is someone who has been there with you since you started out on your journey.

We are so blessed to have a friend who fits each of these definitions. Jesus knows each of us, and we can trust him with our lives. Jesus is the kind of friend we can call to fight every battle. He will be with us through the good and the bad times. Jesus will never leave our side. In our darkest moments, he is there. Jesus is a friend like no other.

Proverbs 18:24 reminds us that there are "friends" who destroy each other, but a real friend sticks closer than a brother. Jesus is this kind of friend. He knows us far better than we even know ourselves. The next time you are experiencing hardship or the pain seems unbearable, I challenge you to call on our friend, the Lord Jesus. He proved the strength of His love for us when He came to earth and gave His life for us.

New Thing

That, however, is not the way of life you learned when you heard about Christ and were taught in him in accordance with the truth that is in Jesus. You were taught, with regard to your former way of life, to put off your old self, which is being corrupted by its deceitful desires; to be made new in the attitude of your minds.
Ephesians 4:20-23 NIV

Sometimes we cling tenaciously to our old ways of doing things, thinking they are the only choices. We may resist anything new or different through indecisiveness; we waiver back and forth between fear and doubt. The word of God tells us in Romans 12, not to copy the behavior and customs of this world, but let God transform you into a new person by changing the way you think. Then you will learn to know God's will for you, which is good, pleasing, and perfect.

Sometimes God calls us to meditate for a time of transformation and healing for the mind, body, and spirit. Once we renew our minds, we can focus on that which God desires of us. He wants to do a new thing in each of our lives, but we must be open and willing to do what God instructs us to do.

June 25

Intimacy with God

And this is the way to have eternal life; to know you, the only true God, and Jesus Christ, the one you sent to earth. John 17:3 NLT

Do you ever feel like you don't have enough energy to get you from one day to the next? Between your work life and your family life you may be stretched so thin that you're very close to breaking. The work that you do is important and you have to contend with being essential but also disposable; necessary but underpaid and overworked. How do you cope?

For non-believers, they seek out stress relievers that come in various forms. As a believer however, we have access to the most therapeutic form of daily renewal in the form of daily devotions and worship. When we enter into the presence of God and worship him in spirit and truth, we leave with a sense of peace. God energizes us to get through each day and focusing on Him, helps us to see the positive in every situation. This mindset reduces stress and anxiety, and improves your overall wellbeing.

God is the greatest physician and healer. He is a friend to those with broken hearts and an aid to those who are burdened. Intimacy with God does so much more for us than we could ever imagine and it is a gift that we should seek every day.

God's Favor

Let love and faithfulness never leave you; bind them around your neck, write them on the tablet of your heart. Then you will win favor and a good name in the sight of God and man.
Proverbs 3:3-4 NIV

God does not play favorites, but in Genesis 6, we are told that Noah found favor with the Lord. God reminds us that he will grant favor according to his will. God's favor is more precious than money.

God chose Mary to be the mother of Jesus. Yes, Mary was favored by God. God could have chosen anyone, but he chose her to fulfill his purpose. Mary must have felt honored that God chose her for such a great responsibility. God will favor us in our jobs, in our churches, and even in our families. God's favor is priceless. We can't pay for favor or even earn it. God blesses us with favor to do his will. When the favor of God is upon you, people won't understand it. Don't make the mistake of trying to explain what God is doing in your life. Rest in assurance that God is moving on your behalf.

June 27

Faithful Promise Keeper

Now there is in store for me the crown of righteousness, which the Lord, the righteous Judge, will award to me on that day—and not only to me but also to all who have longed for his appearing.
2 Timothy 4:8 NIV

Sometimes we pray to God, asking Him to grant our request according to his will. What happens when God does not respond in the time or manner in which we desire. What do we do when the very thing we are trusting God for has not manifested in our lives? How do we handle the disappointment? I'm sure some of us may have even made the mistake of becoming angry with God.

We may be tempted to ask him, "Why are you taking so long? Where are you? Did you forget about me, God?"

God wants to remind us that he has not forgotten us. Hebrews 6:10 says, "For God is not unjust. He will not forget how hard you have worked for him and how you have shown your love to him by caring for other believers as you still do." God has not forgotten about you. Be encouraged today, knowing that there is a greater reward that God has in store for us.

June 28

When God Speaks

In the same way, the Spirit helps us in our weakness. We do not know what we ought to pray for, but the Spirit himself intercedes for us through wordless groans. And he who searches our hearts knows the mind of the Spirit because the Spirit intercedes for God's people in accordance with the will of God. Romans 8:26-27 NIV

God will speak to us when we allow ourselves to press into his presence. God desires a relationship with each of his children. In John 10:27-28, He reminds us that His "sheep listen to my voice. I know them, and they follow me. I give them eternal life, and they will never perish. No one can snatch them away from me."

During our busy days, we should take time to hear God speak. As we care for others, we must never forget the importance of caring for ourselves. There is nothing more important than our spiritual health, and while we tend to the physical needs of others, let us be careful not to neglect this vital part of who we are as believers. Communication with God requires listening and speaking. One of the qualities of effective communication is actively listening and paying close attention to the person who is speaking to you. God wants to talk to each of us, but we have to get silent, be still, and actively listen for His voice.

June 29

A Love Relationship

Whoever claims to love God yet hates a brother or sister is a liar. For whoever does not love their brother and sister, whom they have seen, cannot love God, whom they have not seen.
1 John 4:20 NIV

A love relationship with God is significant in the life of a believer. God commands each of us to love as he loves. When we allow God's love to trump all other emotions in our lives, we can love others freely. Matthew 22:37-38 "Jesus replied, Love the Lord your God with all your heart and with all your soul and with all your mind. This is the first and greatest commandment"

God also commands us to love in John 15:12. He said, "This commandment that you love one another, even as I have loved you." How can we have a love relationship with God but not love those who God commanded us to love? How do we reconcile hating the very people that God sacrificed his son for?

God is love. If we profess to walk with Him but love not our brothers and sisters, then God's truth is not in us. We don't get to pick and choose the parts of the Word that we want to follow to fit them into our World views. We are called to live in love and peace and to represent God in all that we do.

June 30

God's Servant

Then I heard the voice of the Lord saying, "Whom shall I send? And who will go for us?" And I said, Here am I. Send me! Isaiah 6:8 NIV

Being a servant of God requires obedience to do what we are instructed to do. When God works through a servant, anything is possible. We must be available to do whatever he tells us to do. Elijah provides a perfect example of being a servant of God. His name literally translates to "Yahweh is my God" and is indicative of the way Elijah lived his life.

If your life were to determine the name you were given, what would you be called? Is it obvious in everything that you do that you are a servant of God? Do you submit to authority? Do you love those who hate you? Do you pray without ceasing? DO you feed God's sheep?

If all you have is a cross and a bumper sticker saying "Jesus is my friend" then maybe your name would be more about keeping up appearances than serving God. Being God's servant requires a humble spirit that discerns things in the spiritual and in the natural by the guidance of God. A good servant is an obedient servant. A servant who represents his master well and is loyal to him even in his absence.

Search your heart and examine your life up to this point. Have you been God's servant? Could we publicly assign you a new name or would you be too ashamed of what your name would actually reflect, in contrast to who you say you are?

Let us take the time to do the things that God requires from us. Let us treat our salvation with the seriousness it deserves.

July Health Awareness

Juvenile Arthritis Awareness

World Hepatitis Day (July 28)

National Cleft and Craniofacial Awareness and Prevention

July 1

Freedom in Christ

*So Christ has truly set us free. Now make sure that you
stay free, and don't get tied up again in slavery to the law.
Galatians 5:1 NLT*

What do you think of when you think of the word free? Do you think of
something that costs nothing? A free meal…or a free gift? Maybe it makes
you think about liberty. A free country or nation. Or just maybe you think
about personal freedom…the freedom to do whatever you want.

So, if Christ has set us free, what did he set us free from? Verse one suggests
that He came to set us free from the law. Before Christ, the world operated
on the law. The law told God's people how to live and how to properly
worship Him. When Christ came, He fulfilled the law. It was not meant to
be abolished, but to bring the law to fruition. Jesus gave up His freedom, so
that we may have our freedom. We are not slaves to the law; the law is there
to spur us on and help us live a life pointed to Christ. May we be a people
who use our freedom to serve our great King. As we study Galatians 5 and
the fruit of the Spirit over the next month, we will learn about our human
nature and its desires and the Spiritual nature and the fruits of living for the
Lord. Hopefully we will learn about ourselves and how to stay connected to
the source, our great God.

July 2

A Works-Based Faith

For if you are trying to make yourselves right with God by keeping the law, you have been cut off from Christ! You have fallen away from God's grace Galatians 5:4 NLT

Some religions believe that man must earn his way to heaven. They believe that the merit of man paves his way to those pearly gates. This could not be further from the truth. If man's eternal life is based on how good he has been during his early life, then where do we draw the line? How good do you have to be to be good enough? How do you explain the thief on the cross? He certainly wasn't good enough to earn a reservation in heaven.

Our entrance to heave in solely dependent on our faith in Christ. When we accept the gift of grace that God gave us when Christ gave up His freedom on the cross, then we accept His beautiful salvation. We could never be good enough for a perfect and holy God, so God made a way for us to be with Him. Praise Him that He gives us His goodness and mercy so we can be free to follow Him.

July 3

Running the Race

You were running the race so well. Who has held you back from following the truth? It certainly isn't God, for he is the one who called you to freedom. This false teaching is like a little yeast that spreads through the whole batch of dough! Galatians 5:7-9 NLT

Paul wrote the book Galatians to remind the people of the gospel and what Christ had done for them. In these verses, he reminds them of the race they were running that is, the Christian life. However, they had become tied up by the law again and had forgotten the freedom that Christ had given.

We do the same thing, don't we? Many Christians become so concerned with the good they are doing what it looks like, and how people will respond. They become so consumed with WHAT they're doing that they forget WHO they are doing it for.

The truth is that the only way we can run the race well is if we acknowledge who or what is holding us back. Athletes must identify their weaknesses, so they know how to overcome them and succeed. We must see who or what is holding us back from following Christ, so we know how to pursue Him. When we give Him our complete attention, we will find ourselves in a race that has great rewards.

July 4

Life in Freedom

For you have been called to live in freedom, my brothers and sisters. But don't use your freedom to satisfy your sinful nature. Instead, use your freedom to serve one another in love. Galatians 5:13 NLT

Some Christians become consumed with figuring out God's will for their lives. They look for purpose and want to know what God wants from them. Others use their freedom to serve themselves and become wrapped up in what they want for themselves. This verse tells us exactly what God's desire for our lives is: to live freely and use the freedom to serve Him with our lives. Christ gave up His own freedom on the cross, so that we might live to serve Him freely. He wants us to CHOOSE to follow Him. Our calling, our purpose, and His will for our lives, is to live in His freedom. We are not bound by anything in this world. He has freed us so we might live.

He desires us to use the freedom for good, not to satisfy our own sinful natures. If we have been saved and rescued from or sinful desires and use our freedom to fulfill those same desires, then we have become entangled and bound to that sin again: the exact thing that Christ freed us from. Use your freedom for good and serve each other with your freedom.

Love Your Neighbor

For the whole law can be summed up in this one command: "Love your neighbor as yourself." But if you are always biting and devouring one another, watch out! Beware of destroying one another. Galatians 5:14-15 NLT

What a beautiful thought. The entire law that the Galatians tried too hard to follow could be summed up in one simple phrase: Love your neighbor as yourself' Loving others can cover a multitude of sins as it states in 1 Peter 4:8. When we become worried with the law only and forget grace, we neglect loving people. This can turn into judgement and hatred. We begin biting and devouring each other and find ourselves and others destroyed.

However, when we love each other first, we ae able to look past weaknesses, failures, and sins and see the good in people, just like God does with us. Love heals, love endures, and love gives grace. The next time you are tempted toward negativity and gossip, stop and pray and ask God to give you a heart for others. Ask Him to help you forgive, impart grace, and be merciful with others.

July 6

Live by The Spirit

So I say, let the Holy Spirit guide lives. Then you won't be doing what your sinful nature craves. Galatians 5:16 NLT

So how do we live in this amazing freedom and love our neighbor as Galatians 5 tells us? We do exactly what verse 16 says; we allow the Holy Spirit to guide our lives. If you were in an unknown place, a place you had never been before, how would you know where to go? You would need someone or something to help guide you. Maybe you would use a map or GPS. Or maybe you would take the advice of someone who had been there before. That's just what the Holy Spirit does for us. He leads us and guides us in the way we should go.

How do we listen to the Holy Spirit? If you were using a system or person to help guide you, you would read or listen and then follow. In order to allow the Holy Spirit to guide you, you need to read the Bible. Spending deliberate time in the Word will help you learn the ways of the Lord. You need to also spend time in prayer, really listening to what the Spirit is trying to teach you. He will never lead you astray. Through spending time with the Lord, you will draw closer to Him and learn how to follow Him with your whole life.

July 7

Two Natures

The sinful nature wants to do evil, which is just the opposite of what the Spirit wants. And the Spirit gives us desires that are the opposite of what the sinful nature desires. These two forces are constantly fighting each other, so you are not free to carry out your good intentions. Galatians 5:17 NLT

We have two choices to help guide us through this life. We can either allow the Spirit to lead us, or we can be led by our sinful nature. We can't do both. We are either following after the Lord or we are being distracted by the things of this world. This part of Galatians 5 tells us that these two natures are constantly at war with each other. Good versus evil. Righteous versus unrighteousness. Spirit versus sin.

Do you ever feel this spiritual warfare taking place? David said in Psalm 51 that his sin was ever before him. He was aware that even though he wanted to serve the Lord, his sinful nature still took over sometimes. When we are aware of the two natures, we can recognize the evidence of the sin that tries to divert our attention and the fruit that is produced when we keep our eyes on Jesus. Only then will we be able to take measures to make sure our attention stays on the Lord.

July 8

The Sinful Nature

When you follow the desires of your sinful nature, the results are very clear: sexual immorality, impurity, lustful pleasures, idolatry, sorcery, hostility, quarreling, jealousy, outbursts of anger, selfish ambition, dissension, division, envy, drunkenness, wild parties, and other sins like these. Let me tell you again, as I have before, that anyone living that sort of life will not inherit the Kingdom of God. Galatians 5:19-21 NLT

Let's learn a little about the sinful nature so we can recognize it and give those desires over to the Lord. Following the desires of our sinful natures can reap dangerous results. What may seem like a fleeting decision or thought, can turn into something harmful and permanent.

Living in the flesh begins with a thought. One simple thought can give way to an action, and an action can produce a habit. A habit creates a whole different lifestyle. Every one of the results mentioned in the above versus (sexual immorality, impurity, lustful pleasures, idolatry, sorcery, hostility, quarreling, jealousy, outbursts of anger, selfish ambition, dissension, division, envy, drunkenness, wild parties, and other sins like these) come from a tiny thought or desire. For this reason, 2 Corinthians 10:5 tells us to "take every thought captive." The Kingdom of God has no place for people who continuously live a life of rebellion again Him. As Christians our salvation is secure in Christ, but we still must guard ourselves against sins of the flesh so we can be a light in this dark world.

Impurity

When you follow the desires of your sinful nature, the results are very clear: sexual immorality, impurity, lustful pleasures.
Galatians 5:19 NLT

Sexual immorality, impurity, and lustful pleasures are all results of giving into the desires of your sinful nature. David is an example of someone who gave into his sinful desires and caused destruction in his life. It all began with a thought. David saw Bathsheba (another man's wife) bathing on her rooftop and began to desire her. These impure and lustful thoughts gave way to action, when he devised a plot to kill her husband, Uriah. He had her husband killed in battle and took Bathsheba as his wife. His sin had so blinded him that he did even see the destruction he had caused until Nathan began to describe an allegorical situation to him. Nathan helped him see how far he had spiraled as a result of his thoughts and desires.

The Bible says in Matthew 5:28 that when we lust after someone, it's as if we've committed adultery already. David's lusts gave way to an action, and he became so involved that his view of God was completely clouded. We must guard our thoughts against sexual immorality, impurities, and lustful passions that we don't fall into the same destruction as David. May God be our passion and desire.

July 10

Idolatry

Idolatry, sorcery, hostility, quarreling, jealousy, outbursts, selfish ambition, dissension, division. Galatians 5:20 NLT

Idolatry is probably one of the biggest struggles our society has today. We may not worship idols in the way that they did in Bible times, but nonetheless, we create our own gods and worship them like we would worship the one, true God. We make people our gods, material things our gods, and we place value on them that they were never meant to have. We allow these idols to become distractions and even take the throne of God in our lives.

In Exodus 32, Moses had gone up to Mount Sinai and was receiving a word for the Lord when the Israelites turned to idols. They became weary waiting on Moses to come back down the mountain, and ask Aaron to create some gods to lead them. So, they built a gold calf and began worshipping and sacrificing to something that would pass away. This drove a rift between the Israelites and the God who rescued them from Egypt. This happens to us when we place something or someone in the place where God should be. Matthew 6:21 teaches us that where our treasure is, there our hearts will be also. May God be our treasure so can we guard our hearts against idolatry.

July 11

Sorcery/Witchcraft

Idolatry, sorcery, hostility, quarreling, jealousy, outbursts, selfish ambition, dissension, division. Galatians 5:20 NLT

Most people in this world are looking for answers to some pretty big questions. What is the purpose of life? What happens to people when they die? Will I live a full life? Unfortunately, some people try to find their answers in sorcery (mediums, psychics, witchcraft). Webster's Dictionary defines sorcery as "the use of power gained from the assistance or control of evil spirits especially for divining." This is a practice that was evident in Bible times, and is still practiced today. Sorcery is a dangerous practice that places trust in something false than in the true God who does have answers to all of these questions. It is not of the Lord which only means one thing: it is from the king of lies, the Devil.

Isaiah 8:19 tells us that people should inquire of the Lord instead of sorcery. He has all of the answers to every question we seek. Sometimes He didn't give us the answer right away, but He promises us He seeks our good and He knows what we need. He is trustworthy. We don't always need answers to all of the questions. We just need Him.

July 12

Hostility and Quarreling

Idolatry, sorcery, hostility, quarreling, jealousy, outbursts, selfish ambition, dissension, division. Galatians 5:20 NLT

The words hostility and quarreling (arguing) go together. Quarreling produces hostility that divides and destroys relationships, friendships and lives. Proverbs 17:14 says that "starting a quarrel is like spilling water, so drop the dispute before it escalates." What a picture of the destruction that quarreling and hostility can cause! Water spilling can create a mess and all who cross it are at risk of getting hurt.

Think about what happens when we quarrel with others. If we allow it to, quarreling can cause bitterness and anger. Bitterness can destroy us. It causes us to focus on the anger inside of us instead of the things of the Lord. Bitterness can also destroy those around us. Our relationships and friendships can become hostile. One way to avoid quarreling with others starts in your mind. God created all people in His image; if we could view each other as created in the image of God, then maybe we would interact with them differently. Another way is to pray for others. Pray for them to experience the Lord. Prayer not only brings your request to God, but it also changes your mindset. It's hard to be hostile toward someone you are praying for.

July 13

Anger

Idolatry, sorcery, hostility, quarreling, jealousy, outbursts, selfish ambition, dissension, division. Galatians 5:20 NLT

Anger is a natural human emotion. We even see moments of righteous indignation in the Bible when the Israelites would sin against God and even in Christ when the people were degrading the temple. Sin brings about anger in God. Our sinful nature and desires should produce an anger in us that should spur us to pursue righteousness. This verse refers to "outbursts of anger." Webster's Dictionary defines an outburst as "a violent expression of feeling." The moment anger turns violent, it becomes a sin that separates us from God.

Decide today that no one will make you angry. You will control your emotions, and you not entertain angry thoughts. If you begin to feel anger, you will actively seek the Lord. Pray in the moment for the Lord to comfort you and give you His peace that passes all understanding (Philippians 4:7)

July 14

Selfishness

Idolatry, sorcery, hostility, quarreling, jealousy, outbursts, selfish ambition, dissension, division. Galatians 5:20 NLT

Philippians 2:3 teaches to do nothing out of selfish ambition or vain conceit. Selfishness means putting yourself above others, your own welfare, and disregarding others. A selfish life looks at what he needs to do to further himself, to bring benefit to himself, seek his own rewards. Selfishness puts no value in someone else's life, but places great value in his own life.

This verse in Philippians goes on to say that instead, you ought to, in humility, think of others as better than yourself. This what a selfless life does. A selfless life puts others lives above his own. A selfless life places great value in someone else's life. Jesus was the greatest example of a selfless life. Jesus, in placing great value in our lives and salvation, gave up His divine privilege and humbled himself in obedience to God and died a criminal's death on the cross (Philippians 2:7-8). So, we ought to value others and cling to humility over selfish ambition. We have a God who did the same for us.

Disagreement and Division

Idolatry, sorcery, hostility, quarreling, jealousy, outbursts, selfish ambition, dissension, division. Galatians 5:20 NLT

Hostility and quarreling lead to dissension and division. Remember that everything begins with a thought. So, our thoughts about others or their viewpoints can lead to quarreling. If quarreling continues, it produces dissension or contentious quarreling. The devil is really good at stirring up trouble among the church and Christian people. If we do nothing to stop the quarreling, this eventually brings about division, which is exactly what the enemy wants. We can't lead others to the Lord if we are standing against each other.

So how can we guard ourselves against dissension and division as a people and as a church? It begins with each one of us. If we all see each other as images of God, just like we discussed Day 12, and if we seek unity together, then we will stand together as one force against the devil. We will be a force to be reckoned with.

July 16

Jealousy and Envy

Idolatry, sorcery, hostility, quarreling, jealousy, outbursts, selfish ambition, dissension, division. Galatians 5:20 NLT

The words jealousy and envy are often used synonymously, but they are each mentioned in these verses. They mean something a little different, but stem from the same feeling: dissatisfaction with one's own self. Jealousy is resentment toward someone else for taking something or having something you once had, and envy is wanting something someone else has that you don't. joseph and his brothers are an example of this in Genesis 37. Joseph was his father's favorite son and was shown favoritism often. His brothers became very resentful toward joseph when he tried to explain his dream to them about how they would serve him in the future. Just like some of the other sinful desires, their jealousy and envy began as a thought, which produced an action. They devised a plan to get rid of joseph. Remember that an action gives way to a habit which creates a lifestyle? Well, throughout the brothers lives they become hostile, and they sin toward others. When we see them in Genesis 43-45, they travel to Egypt to beg for food from one of Egypt's rulers, who happens to be joseph in disguise. Everything happened as he had predicted and according to God's plan. The brothers allowed their bitterness to rule over them and lived with it for years.

The beautiful part of the story of joseph is the forgiveness he found for his brothers and the reconciliation the brothers found. Even when we give in to sinful desires such as jealousy or envy, God can still repair what was broken. Pray and ask God to give you strength to not give into these feelings or to heal what has been if your feelings have already done damage.

Drunkenness and Wild Parties

Envy, drunkenness, wild parties, and other sins like these. Let me tell you again, as I have before, that anyone living that sort of life will not inherit the Kingdom of God. Galatians 5:21 NLT

Our freedom gives us the opportunity to live without chains or bound to anything. 1 Corinthians 10:23 says that everything is permissible (or "I am allowed to do anything as the NLT version says). So, one might ask, "Anything?" Remember, that we do not live as those under the law, but free in Christ. However, verse 23 goes on to say that not everything is beneficial. Some Christians use their salvation as a license to live without restrictions. In this case, they end up looking no different than the world. Someone who becomes entangled with drunkenness and wild parties is not someone living in their freedom, but someone who is bound by their sin. This verse in Galatians 5:21 says, that person will not inherit the Kingdom of God. We cannot claim to love Christ and deny Him by the way that we live.

If you are someone who has lived this type of lifestyle or fell away, there is always hope. God's grace is more than enough to cover ALL of your sins. Pray that God will help you live in your freedom and not give in to the slavery of sin.

July 18

The Spiritual Nature

But the Holy Spirit produces this kind of fruit in our lives.
Galatians 5:22a NLT

We were both with human nature. This is the side of us that makes humanly choices to benefit ourselves. We learn the word "no" at a very early age and learn to communicate when we need something. As we grow, we start to test right from wrong, learning good versus evil. The moment we become a Christian, God places the Holy Spirit to live and breathe inside of us, transforming our lives completely. We now have his guidance and a spiritual nature. When we live for the Lord and His righteousness, the Holy Spirit will produce fruit in our lives. God plants the seed of the gospel in our hearts and it grows and bears fruit for all to see if we allow Him to do His work.

The fruit of the Spirit is the evidence of Christ's salvation in our hearts and God working in our lives if we are bearing fruit, then those around us will know we are saved. Matthew 7:17 says that a good tree will bear good fruit and a bad tree will produce bad fruit. It goes on to say in verse 18 that a good tree cannot produce bad fruit and a bad tree cannot produce good fruit. So, we will be known by our fruits. If we love the Lord and strive to live a life following Christ, then we will produce good fruit.

The Fruit of Love

But the Holy Spirit produces this kind of fruit in our lives:
love, joy, peace, patience, kindness, goodness, faithfulness.
Galatians 5:22 NLT

Love is the opposite of every one of the sinful desires. Sexual immorality, impurity, and lust are all temporary and damaging, while love is eternal and everlasting. Anger and bitterness are divisive and destroy lives, while love sees past imperfections and arguments, and heals all who come in its path. Jealousy and envy seek to destroy the heart and pollute the mind, while love is selfless and sees past earthly possessions.

That's why there is an entire book in the Bible (Song of Solomon) devoted to Eros love (a passionate godly kind of love). That's why there is an entire chapter devoted to Agape love (1 Corinthians 13) teaching us how to really love those around us and those we meet with a godly love. And that's why there are countless stories about Phileo love (friendship) such as Jonathan and David in 1 Samuel 18. 1 Corinthians 13:13 states that "three things will last forever-faith, hope, and love-and the greatest of these is love." Love is so great that it can replace those sinful desires with a desire to follow Christ. Put your hope in His powerful love.

July 20

The Fruit of Joy

But the Holy Spirit produces this kind of fruit in our lives:
love, joy, peace, patience, kindness, goodness, faithfulness.
Galatians 5:22 NLT

Joy is often seen as synonymous to the word happiness. But it is so much different than the temporary feeling of happiness we were created with. Our happiness is completely dependent on our circumstances. If everything is going really well, then we will feel happiness. That happiness can change in an instant. One minute we're happy, on top of the clouds, and the next minute we are down in the dumps, feeling sorry for ourselves. Sometimes it can even change with the weather! Joy is so much more than that temporary feeling. One definition Webster's Dictionary uses is "a source or cause for delight." That's exactly why Biblical joy is. The fruit of joy LIVES in us. It CAUSES us to hope and have faith. It is a SOURCE.

Nehemiah 8:10b says, "Don't be dejected and sad, for the joy of the LORD is your strength." His joy is our strength! That means that even when we feel weak or don't feel happy, we have His joy giving us our next breath.

The Fruit of Peace

*But the Holy Spirit produces this kind of fruit in our lives:
love, joy, peace, patience, kindness, goodness, faithfulness.
Galatians 5:22 NLT*

The word "peace" tends to have many different meanings. It is something that some people strive to have and others do everything they can to avoid it. Some try to "keep the peace" more than they try to live and peaceful heart. Keeping the peace just means you are trying to make sure others don't disturb you. That's not really the fruit of peace, now is it?

The Hebrew word for peace is shalom. According to Encylopedia.com it means totality or completeness, success, fulfillment, wholeness, harmony, security, and well-being. Peace is all of that wrapped into one word. Let's focus on a few of these meanings. If we really know God, then we are complete, we are whole, needing nothing a lacking nothing. He had fulfilled or satisfied our every need. We find our security and our well-being in Him. For from Him, for Him, and in Him we find our peace. If we truly find our peace in Him, then we understand in Philippians 4:7 when Paul says, "Then you will experience God's peace, which exceeds anything we can understand. His peace will guard your hearts and minds as you live in Christ Jesus."

July 22

The Fruit of Patience

But the Holy Spirit produces this kind of fruit in our lives:
love, joy, peace, patience, kindness, goodness, faithfulness.
Galatians 5:22 NLT

What does the word patience look like to you? Does it look like a child waiting on Christmas? Or a family waiting to see their loved ones? Or how about a working waiting on his wages? In the Bible, Jacob wanted for 14 years to marry his bride Rachel. Joshua waited to walk into the promised land. Mary waited for her sweet baby boy to be born. Many times, we think of temporary examples when we think of patience. There are some things that just aren't quick moments of patience. Our salvation is one of those things. The Bible tells us we will see our salvation come to fruition when this life is over. We will wait our entire lives on the Lord and His promises. Sometimes His promises are fulfilled quickly and other times it feels like forever. The King James Version of the Bible calls the word patience "long suffering" and that's what it feels like at times.

However, we can be sure that God ALWAYS fulfills His promises and the waiting is ALWAYS worth it. There are blessings to be found in the waiting. We find friendships, relationships and sweet fellowship with the Lord when we wait patiently on Him.

July 23

The Fruit of Kindness

But the Holy Spirit produces this kind of fruit in our lives:
love, joy, peace, patience, kindness, goodness, faithfulness.
Galatians 5:22 NLT

There was time in our world, not too long ago, when people would go to the video store on a Friday night to rent a VHS. Every video had the same message on it: "Be kind. Please rewind." When you finished watching your video, if you were a kind person, you would rewind your tape to get it ready for the next person. It was always frustrating receiving a video that hadn't been rewound. You were doing something kind that would affect the next person.

Isn't that what kindness is anyway? Anything nice we do that affects someone else? Sometimes kind is a small gesture: a card, a thank you, an invitation. Sometimes it is much larger: a donation, a gift, a mission. Jesus lived His life on earth being kind to those around Him. He ate with the sinners. He healed the broken. He listened to the little children. He was completely selfless. That's what kind is. It is denying yourself and putting someone else's needs and well-being above your own. All it takes is one thought, one gesture. Maybe these gestures will become a habit and in turn produce a lifestyle of kindness.

July 24

The Fruit of Goodness

But the Holy Spirit produces this kind of fruit in our lives:
love, joy, peace, patience, kindness, goodness, faithfulness.
Galatians 5:22 NLT

It can be difficult at times to find good in the world. War, tragedy, divorce, disasters, and crime can cloud our view of what good is. When Adam and Eve disobeyed God, sin entered the world. From then on, sin separated us from God and has always been at war with good. However, God's goodness drives out all evil. It is the light in the darkness; it overtakes the darkness.

David understood the goodness of God. In Psalm 23:6, he said, "Surely your goodness and unfailing love will pursue me all the days of my life, and I will live in the house of the Lord forever. Goodness doesn't save us, but it's the fruit of His salvation and pursues us when we know God. Jesus came to save man from sin and evil doing, and He placed His goodness in our hearts. With His goodness, we can impact the lives of others. We can bless others because He has blessed us with so much.

July 25

The Fruit of Faithfulness

But the Holy Spirit produces this kind of fruit in our lives:
love, joy, peace, patience, kindness, goodness, faithfulness.
Galatians 5:22 NLT

God's faithfulness is one of His best qualities. It is unlike anything man can do. No matter how hard we try, we can never be completely faithful, not to our family, not to our friends, and definitely not to ourselves. We are a wandering people. We become distracted at the first sign of something shinier and prettier than what we already have. Even when man fails, God continues to be faithful because it is not in His nature to be unfaithful. He simply cannot unfaithful.

So how can we be faithful when our human nature is so wrapped up in ourselves? The answer is our spiritual nature. When our source is God and we are connected to that source through prayer and Bible study, then we will experience the fruit of the Spirit: faithfulness. Simply put, we can be faithful because God is faithful. His faithfulness can reign in or lives.

July 26

The Fruit of Gentleness

Gentleness, and self-control. There is no law against these things!
Galatians 5:23 NLT

1 Peter 3:4 tells us we should "clothe ourselves with the unfailing beauty of a gentle and quiet spirit. This is precious to God." Just like we put on clothes in the morning before we start our day we should put on gentleness. Like the others, this is a fruit of the Spirit you can see on the outside. That's why we should put it on. The people around us will see whatever we put on. So, if we put on bitterness, harsh words, or anger, that is what people will see.

When we use gentle words and actions toward others, we affect the way they view us and the way they view Christianity. Since we bear the name of Christ, we need to clothe ourselves with gentleness. Show others the kind of gentle words and actions you would want from them.

The Fruit of Self-Control

Gentleness, and self-control. There is no law against these things!
Galatians 5:23 NLT

The opposite of all of the sinful desires we've studied is self-control. While the desires of our human nature are impulsive and destructive, the spiritual nature is careful, gracious, and operates under self-control. Think of this example, a vulgar mouth is unhinged and curses everything that comes in its path because it is controlled by the sinful nature. James 3:6 calls the tongue speaks with goodness and gentleness. With it we can bless and worship God, but it takes self-control. James 3:2 says that if we can control the tongue, then we control ourselves in every other way.

We can have self-control with our bodies when we submit our bodies over the Lord and allow the Holy Spirit control of our lives. See, then it is not our human nature in control, but our Spiritual nature leading and guiding us. Sometimes that means offering parts of us that we haven't given over to Him, and other times it means offering all of us.

July 28

No Law Against These

Gentleness, and self-control. There is no law against these things!
Galatians 5:23 NLT

It is hard to imagine a world without law and order. Everything requires some sort of order. Countries require a rule of law to govern their societies. Families must have rules in place to help raise and discipline their children. Driving requires rules to stay safe. There are laws against the sins of the flesh. Every one of them has a consequence or can lead to dangerous lifestyles.

But there are no laws against the spiritual nature and the fruit of the spirit. NO LAWS! There is no limit to how much love we can show, how much kindness we can give, or how much goodness we can bestow on others! There are no laws against these things because at the depths of the fruit of the Spirit is the gospel, and salvation is a free gift to us from God our Father.

July 29

Nailed to The Cross

Those who belong to Christ Jesus have nailed the passions and desires of their sinful nature to his cross and crucified them there.
Galatians 5:24 NLT

So, what do we do with these sinful desires? We know that even after we're saved, we still struggle from time to time with the desires of our human nature. Like we've already studied, these desires begin as thoughts, give way to actions, produce habits, and create lifestyles. They threaten to take everything away from us. So, we must not entertain even a small thought.

If you belong to Christ Jesus, meaning you have recognized your sin and the depths of your human nature, asked for forgiveness, and now live in His freedom, then you have access to the cross by way of the Holy Spirit! When Jesus died on the cross for our sins, He nailed every one of them up there! So, when you struggle with the sins of your former life, remember that when you gave your life to Christ; He nailed every sin and struggle to the cross. He crucified them once and for all. You don't have to live as a slave to your human nature. You live in the freedom of the Spirit!

July 30

Follow the Spirit

Since we are living by the Spirit, let us follow the Spirit's leading in every part of our lives. Galatians 5:25 NLT

The Holy Spirit is not only our spiritual guide like we have already studied, but He holds the map. He knows the unknown territory that is life. With Him as our guide, we can place confidence in His leading. Have you ever tried to figure out how to put something together without a guide or instructions? It takes twice as long to put it together and many times we do something wrong and cause it not to work. Our lives are a lot like that. If we try to make our own decisions without the leading and guiding of the Holy Spirit, then we fail and make a mess of things. The Holy Spirit helps us make decisions and leads our hearts to the Father.

This scripture doesn't say to give part of your life to the Lord for His leading, but EVERY part of our lives. He has given us the Holy Spirit to live in our hearts so that we would follow His leading. He is a good Father and knows what's good for us better than we ever could.

July 31

Be Compassionate, Be Unified

Let us not become conceited, or provoke one another, or be jealous of one another. Galatians 5:26 NLT

As a church, the greatest thing we can do for each other and for God is to stand together, in unity 1 Corinthians 1:10 tells us, "to live in harmony with each other. Let there be no divisions in the church. Rather, be of one mind, united in thought and purpose." Imagine what the church can accomplish when we are of one mind and united in everything we think and do? We can do this when we are living in the Spirit!

This was the mindset of the church in Acts 2. They were so filled with the Holy Spirit, that verse 42 says they were devoted to the teaching of the Word, the fellowship of believers, and the sharing of meals. They sold their possessions, met daily, and took care of those in need. What was the result of this Spirit-filled living? Verse 47 tells us that the Lord was adding to their fellowship those who were being saved EVERY SINGLE DAY. Acts 2 shows us the entire purpose of the church. So, believers, let's start living in the Spirit, treating each other with love and respect, and meeting together in unity, so we can experience everything that God has for us!

August Health Awareness

National Breast-Feeding Month

National Immunization Awareness

Psoriasis Awareness

World Breast Feeding Week (August 1-7)

August 1

Depend on The Holy Spirit

And I will ask the Father, and he will give you another Advocate,
who will never leave you. John 14:16 NLT

It is a known fact that working in healthcare as a nurse is a very demanding job; not only does it take a toll on one's physical health, it is also mentally exhausting. Nurses are the unseen backbones of the medical and health systems. We are life-savers. The life of a nurse is not easy. Daily, we face incessant demands from sick and dying patients. We work long hours, keeping sleepless nights, at the same time, communicating with the doctors to meet patients' needs. We can say nurses wear many hats. To perform to one's full potentials and capacities, especially as a Christian, we need the help of the Holy Spirit. Situations come to test our faith, and work pressure tests our patience. We really do not need to wait for things to get out of hand before we call on the Holy Spirit. The Holy Spirit is our helper; we need to rely on Him daily to help us become better nurses and friends to our patients.

August 2

Let Love Lead

Owe nothing to anyone—except for your obligation to love one another. If you love your neighbor, you will fulfill the requirements of God's law. Romans 13:8 NLT

One of the greatest commandments in the Bible is, "Love one another." As spirit-filled Christians who rely on the Holy Spirit for daily direction and inspiration, we should work in love because love is the fruit of the Holy Spirit. Love is the greatest gift we can give to humanity. Love has healing power. When the patients are treated with love and kindness, it helps them to recuperate faster. Showing love to our patients includes saying a word of prayer with them, motivating them to take their medications, helping them through their recovery, and reassuring them of the healing power of God.

August 3

Nursing Is A Calling

You didn't choose me. I chose you. I appointed you to go and produce lasting fruit, so that the Father will give you whatever you ask for, using my name. John 15:16 NLT

Our place of work is not just a place we go to make money; rather, it is our place of assignment. We are God's representatives here on earth; therefore, everything we do should reflect the nature of God. Being a nurse is not just a profession, it is a calling to care for the sick. Every nurse is a channel of God's blessing and healing. When carrying out clinical duties, we should always have it at the back of mind that there's a human spirit God has placed in front of us. Nurses are called to medical ministry, to be used as God's healing hands to the sick and ailing.

August 4

You Are the Light

In the same way, let your good deeds shine out for all to see, so that everyone will praise your heavenly Father. Matthew 5:16 NLT

Working in healthcare requires that we work with people as they go through difficult and vulnerable times. The near-death situations that patients face can cause the patient to doubt the existence or the goodness of God. As a nurse, we find ourselves being a shoulder to cry on and a listening ear. It is imperative that we let our light shine—we are the light in the darkness.

August 5

Start Your Day with Prayer

And we are confident that he hears us whenever we ask for anything that pleases him. 1 John 5:14 NLT

One of the remarkable activities that mark a believer's day is the time for prayers. In praying, we communicate with our Maker and loving Father in heaven. But we do not just rush down on our knees, tell Him all we want Him to do for us, and zoom off for the day's business. When we pray, we communicate deeply with God. We are free to bare our fears, our expectations, the yearnings of our hearts, and the prospects of our future. When a patient is on a sickbed, there is a need for proper communication with the healthcare personnel. The patient reports every improvement or relapse in their body. They bare their hearts, seeking comfort from their fears and the assurance that all will be well. In like manner, God waits for us at the altar of prayer. Although He knows it all, yet He expects us to come and tell Him how far we have come, and then draw strength from Him.

August 6

Unshakable Faith

The righteous person faces many troubles, but the LORD comes to the rescue each time. Psalm 34:19 NLT

Daily, we find ourselves in situations that question our beliefs. This is especially so when your line of work puts you directly in the middle of such demands. Take the case of a nurse who comes to work to see good people in pain, and probably some professed believers struggling through the most terminal of diseases. It takes more than a simple belief to still cling to the promises of God for our lives after that. It takes an unshakeable faith. The truth is, everyone's faith gets tested at one point or the other in their lives. When situations like this come to sieve you and stretch your belief in God, it will be the time to dig on your heels and totally depend on Him, notwithstanding the prevailing situation we see with our eyes and analyze with the senses. Faith always manifests in doggedness, resilience, and absolute trust in God. The more we focus on Jesus and His promises to us in the scriptures, the more we draw strength from Him and become energized to overcome these tests of faith.

August 7

Learn to Show Empathy

Since God chose you to be the holy people he loves, you must clothe yourselves with tenderhearted mercy, kindness, humility, gentleness, and patience. Colossians 3:12 NLT

Today, it can be said that the world is losing its milk of kindness and empathy. Daily, the media is overwhelmed with acts of wickedness, bloodshed, and man's inhumanity to man. However, in the midst of it all, we should not lose our identities as Christians. When Christ walked the earth, He was quick to show compassion to the sick, and so He healed them and freed many who were under the oppression of foul spirits. Today, we are the called; we are the Church and body of Christ on earth. We represent Him and bear witness of the One whose compassion is limitless. So, wherever we go, and in whatsoever we do, we show empathy to those who are in pain, suffering, bereaved, and to those who need help. We bear the torch of humanity and live true to the One who has called us according to His purpose. If and when we lack compassion and empathy, then it is time to retrace our steps and find out where we missed it. Our Father will be ever there, arms outstretched to lead us on.

August 8

God Cares

How precious are your thoughts about me, O God. They cannot be numbered! I can't even count them; they outnumber the grains of sand! And when I wake up, you are still with me! Psalm 139:17-18 NLT

Taking care of the sick and invalid is a special job and one that will usually put anybody under pressure. Aside from the basic demand of taking care of the sick and the injured, there are the demands of monitoring the patients, safe administration of medications, patients' protection, healthcare guides, and clear explanations of the patient's condition to the family. Everyone expects the nurse to care for them and attend to every of their health needs and challenges, and very few have ever taken the time to ask the nurse how she is faring.

But there is good news! When no one seems to care about how you fare; when friends and family assume you are doing just fine and appear not to care; when we strain under the weight of caring for the weak; we know that we have someone who really cares about us too!

God cares about us. In life, we may feel that we are not important and we may appear insignificant, God cares about the tiniest details of our lives. He is always there to guide our hands, to help us say the right words, and to keep us safe in all.

August 9

God's Mercy

So let us come boldly to the throne of our gracious God. There we will receive his mercy, and we will find grace to help us when we need it most. Hebrews 4:16 NLT

The patients on the sick bed are always looking out for mercy; some are in pains and dire situations, battling with terminal diseases. Sometimes all patients need is a word of encouragement. The Bible says, "Blessed are the merciful for they shall obtain mercy!" Therefore, showing mercy to others helps us also obtain mercy from God. This is not the time to be mean, infuriated, or upset because of the demands that come with the job. God wants to reach out daily to the sick and show them His mercy, but that can only be done when they see God through our eyes. Being merciful requires that we have a large heart. Nurses should always listen with their hearts, not just their ears. Medical staff should treat all patients as if they were family members.

You Are A Special Gift from God

For we are God's masterpiece. He has created us anew in Christ Jesus, so we can do the good things he planned for us long ago.
Ephesians 2:10 NLT

Nurses are special gifts to humanity from God. Their impact in the world cannot be overemphasized. For most people, nursing is not a dream career because they cannot withstand seeing someone else's blood, urine, or vomits. It takes a person with a large heart to be a nurse; it takes a special person to be a nurse. Juggling a lot of responsibilities can be very overwhelming. Understand that you are a priceless jewel. Remember, your uniqueness and your caring heart are more than gold. Sometimes situations you might have to deal with rude patients and difficult coworkers; this is not to feel small or belittled. Instead, we should remember our impact on the world. Today, let us see ourselves in God's eyes, as a precious and priceless gift to humanity. A person who is valuable and great, and who leaves tremendous impacts on their world.

God Compensates

Work willingly at whatever you do, as though you were working for the Lord rather than for people. Remember that the Lord will give you an inheritance as your reward, and that the Master you are serving is Christ. Colossians 3:23-24 NLT

All through history, God always compensates His people in grand style. We have seen several stories in the Bible of how God compensates His diligent servants. We should not feel that our labor for humanity is all in vain. While nursing can be a very demanding career, it can also be a rewarding one, especially because God is the rewarder. God is watching every good deed that we do. The times we took a patient's case in prayers as if they were related to us; the times we lent a helping hand; the times we encouraged a dying patient to keep on the faith, those little moments all count. Sometimes the devil might whisper to us that if we had taken the easier way or compromised on our godly standards, things would have been better. That's not true. Let us continue to work in love, integrity, and faithfulness to the call. God has promised to pay us back for all the sacrifices.

The Holy Spirit Is Our Strengthener

For I can do everything through Christ, who gives me strength.
Philippians 4:13 NLT

Every human being experiences fatigue and burnout at some point in their lives. The nursing profession is not left out. The caregiver also needs care—they go through physical and emotional burnout. The long shifts can be very detrimental to their entire wellbeing. Shift-work increases the chance of being worked up, which can lead to fatigue-related errors. And errors are, of course, detrimental to the health of the patients. When we experience burnout, we should remember that we are never alone; we should then take some rest and depend on the supernatural strength from the Holy Spirit. The Bible reminds us that the Holy Spirit is our strength when we are weak. Simply call on the Holy Spirit for help, you will receive supernatural strength.

August 13

Wisdom of God

But the wisdom from above is first of all pure. It is also peace loving, gentle at all times, and willing to yield to others. It is full of mercy and good deeds. It shows no favoritism and is always sincere. James 3:17 NLT

In life, generally, we all need the wisdom to deal with the daily challenges that we encounter. One of the most sensitive areas, as healthcare personnel, is dealing with difficult patients. People come to us with all kinds of issues. The Bible says that wisdom is profitable to direct; therefore, we should depend on the wisdom of God to handle situations that are beyond our control. It takes wisdom to have a healthy relationship with people who take our services for granted. It takes wisdom to be nice when someone is rude and unappreciative toward us. Wisdom is the only way to handle all relationships; we need to ask God to give us wisdom every day to overcome challenges.

Laying of Hands

As the sun went down that evening, people throughout the village brought sick family members to Jesus. No matter what their diseases were, the touch of his hand healed every one. Luke 4:40 NLT

All through the time in the hospital, nurses use their hands from the tiniest thing to the greatest. They administer drugs, give injections, and check body temperatures. When they assist during surgery, their hands are always in use. Nurses are always out and about using their hands. Our hands are God's instruments. It should be sanctified and blessed to bring perfect healing. As Christians, we have been given the power to lay hands on the sick and ask God for His healing power. More than just administering treatments, we are carrying the power of God to heal the sick and raise the dead. Each time we are on duty, let's exercise our faith in healing through the use of our hands.

August 15

Abstaining from Sin

The temptations in your life are no different from what others experience. And God is faithful. He will not allow the temptation to be more than you can stand. When you are tempted, he will show you a way out so that you can endure.
1 Corinthians 10:13 NLT

When we are living in sin, and it becomes a hindrance for the Holy Spirit to live in us and work through us. Every day as we resume duty, we should ask God for the forgiveness of sins. No matter how we try to live a holy life and abstain from immorality, there are some sins that we still commit unknowingly. Sometimes it can be how we react to situations, and at other times, it can be in our conversations. We can commit sin unknowingly and unconsciously. Every day has its own challenges, so let us always ask for the grace to abstain from sin and the grace to be filled with the Holy Spirit to fulfill our assignment.

August 16

God's Direction

Seek his will in all you do, and he will show you which path to take. Proverbs 3:6 NLT

We all need directions in our lives. We need to know what to do at the right time, and what not to do. We need direction on where to go and where not to go. God wants us to totally trust in Him to direct us—He can only be our best director. Before we go about our clinical duties, let's seek divine directions. In other not to make mistakes that can endanger a patient's life, we should always seek God's direction. Harken to the voice of God and pray to Him for directions. God speaks to us daily. We are taught that we can hear the voice of God in several ways: through people, through dreams, visions, the Word of God, and, most importantly, through the Holy Spirit.

August 17

Obedience to God

Stay on the path that the LORD your God has commanded you to follow. Then you will live long and prosperous lives in the land you are about to enter and occupy. Deuteronomy 5:33 NLT

God gives us instructions and commandments because He loves us, and He wants us to enjoy all He has already given. When He places boundaries and restricts us from certain things, it is more about protecting us. Therefore, our obedience should not be based on getting a reward from God because our obedience favors us and not God. For instance, the Holy Spirit may prompt us to go out of our way to help a patient financially, but we may object. That is not being obedient. Obedience is not a bribe to God. We are not trying to cajole Him whatsoever. He wants us to obey so we can get the best out of life and all He has already done for us.

August 18

Feed on God's Word

I will meditate in thy precepts, and have respect unto thy ways.
Psalm 119:15 NLT

The Word of God is life; it is power, and it is truth. The Word of God nourishes our souls. Before resuming duty, we should open our Bible to study the Word of God. There is no better way to navigate this life outside studying the Bible. Jesus told us that we should not live by bread alone. This is very true in our generation when most people are hunting for money. There is always a need to meet, but Jesus continues to remind us that this life is not our home—it is temporary. We should depend on the Word of God and be more concerned with the kingdom of God. When we make it a habit to study the Bible to know the Word of God, we build our faith and equip our minds to win the gimmicks of the devil. We can also minister to the patients. We can assure the sick that God heals; tell the sad and depressed that indeed God comforts.

August 19

Standing on The Promises of God

Reassure me of your promise, made to those who fear you.
Psalm 119:38 NLT

A promise is a declaration or assurance that one will do something or that a particular thing will happen. As Christians, we always have our expectations from God. Standing on God's promises includes joining our faith with others for the restoration of health. Perhaps we have told a patient to trust God for healing, and the health is rather deteriorating. We are asked severally where our God is, or we have personal and silent battles we don't share with anyone. Do not despair! This is the time to trust God even more for the fulfillment of His promises. Let's have confidence that God will always come through for us at all times.

August 20

Our Help Comes from God

Even strong young lions sometimes go hungry, but those who trust in the LORD will lack no good thing. Psalm 34:10 NLT

God continuously reaches out to help us. He ordained us to be on earth as a caregiver at a crucial time as this. There's nothing we are going through that God is not aware of. God is a good Father; He is loving and caring. He loves us indeed, and we are still alive today because of His love, mercy, and grace. God is connected to us; He is only watching if we will connect to Him. Imagine if we are always reaching out to Him the way we stay on our phones, we will never be stranded. The way He wants us to help the sick is the same way He wants to help us to meet our personal needs.

He Is Concerned About You

Your righteousness is like the mighty mountains, your justice like the ocean depths. You care for people and animals alike, O LORD.
Psalm 36:6 NLT

The Bible reminds us of the beautiful relationship Jesus had with Lazarus and his two sisters, Martha and Mary. He often visited their house in Bethany to rest. Unfortunately, a tragedy occurred. Lazarus fell ill and, unfortunately, died. Jesus arrived to see that His friend was dead, and his sisters were in distress, devastated, and wailing over their dead brother. Jesus cried out of compassion, and He performed a miracle by raising their dead brother to life. In like manner, Jesus isn't indifferent to the situations we face. His compassion is endless. He will miraculously raise the dead situations we encounter. Jesus is concerned about us; He hasn't changed. His compassion is still the same.

August 22

You Are Planted by The Riverside

They are like trees planted along the riverbank, bearing fruit each season. Their leaves never wither, and they prosper in all they do.
Psalm 1:3 NLT

In Psalm 1, God draws the comparison between those that follow Him, to the tree that is planted by the riverside, which bears fruit in season and out of season. But that is if we meditate on His Word and follow His leading. Perhaps, we sometimes feel tired, parched, lifeless, and empty, especially after a night shift with so many demanding patients. We should see ourselves as coming out stronger regardless of the challenges. We should believe in the Word of God that, like a tree planted by the riverside, our leaves shall not wither. The river represents the Holy Spirit who desires to flow into and through our lives and spread to others.

August 23

Avoid Comparison

Pay careful attention to your own work, for then you will get the satisfaction of a job well done, and you won't need to compare yourself to anyone else. For we are each responsible for our own conduct. Galatians 6:4-5 NLT

We often hear that the "grass is greener on the other side". We imagine that our neighbors have everything together. We may feel like our colleague has their life all figured out, and the other has better qualifications. Funny how we only see the good things in others and the wrong things in ourselves. Comparing oneself to others compromises one's future. We need to accept and love ourselves as we are created, which includes our strengths and weaknesses. That way, we can accept the patients as they come into our lives at different points.

Be Sensitive to The Needs of Others.

God knows how often I pray for you. Day and night I bring you and your needs in prayer to God, whom I serve with all my heart by spreading the Good News about his Son. Romans 1:9 NLT

Being sensitive to the needs of those around us requires that we become selfless. Sometime our friends or colleagues could be going through some family issues, the patient on the sick bed might have some emotional needs, and we just might be the right person that God could use to meet those needs. When we go about our clinical duties or when spending time with our family or friends, we should ask the Holy Spirit to help us discern if those around us are carrying problems that are too much for them to bear all alone. If we realize that they're weighed down, ask them: "What's happening in your life? How can I pray for you today?" God could use us to lighten their load. We can simply lend a listening ear. Listening to God's voice before speaking will help soothe the listener. It is God's way of using us to help someone else along the journey.

Making Jesus Our Model

Then Jesus said to his disciples, "If any of you wants to be my follower, you must turn from your selfish ways, take up your cross, and follow me. Matthew 16:24 NLT

For every time Jesus was mentioned in the Bible, we saw that He went about doing good, raising the dead, healing the sick, setting the captives free, and bringing restorations to the helpless. Our role model is Jesus. The healthcare center is a place to show our examples as followers of Christ. For the good things that Jesus did, we have the power to do the same and much more as we have the Holy Spirit. When we walk around, people should say good things about us and glorify Jesus.

Whether it is attending to patients, relating with our colleagues, spending time with family, our attitude should reflect how Jesus would treat the people around him.

August 26

The Impossibility Specialist

For nothing is impossible with God. Luke 1:37 NLT

God is saying whatever is impossible with a man will be made possible by Him. What are your expectations? What is in your life that looks impossible? God is saying He will make it possible if you involve Him in the whole equation. We always have something troubling us; life is full of so many issues to deal with. We cannot get any breakthrough, deliverance, healing, or blessings from God without faith in His possibilities. If there are things, we may have tried to do in the past that didn't work, God is saying to us to try again this time by faith! God is giving you the tongue of the learned and awakening your heart to wisdom.

August 27

When You Do Not Feel Like Praying

For his anger lasts only a moment, but his favor lasts a lifetime! Weeping may last through the night, but joy comes with the morning. Psalm 30:5 NLT

In some seasons, we struggle with our prayer life. It happens to most of us. We may not feel like praying. We may feel we've had enough of repeating the same things and not noticing any change. Maybe we noticed some progress, but in other areas of our life, we lament the stagnation, the fact that we are still struggling with the same weaknesses, repeating the same failures. We're a people of hope, aspirations, prayers, and struggles, full of good intentions but so weak. We have great days, weeks, sometimes even months and years...and suddenly, the crash comes. When this happens, we should have confidence that God will never abandon us. We should study and meditate on the Word of God.

August 28

Attitude When Waiting

I am worn out waiting for your rescue, but I have put my hope in your word. Psalm 119:81 NLT

Our attitude can set the mood for anything in life. If we're happy and content, the world is our playground. But if things are not right with the world, there's trouble lying in wait for someone. Regardless of what is happening in our lives, what is your attitude as you wait for relief? Are you frantic or worried? Or are you resting in the arms of Jesus that He will work everything out? Your attitude while waiting is imperative on how you view your current situation. Change your focus from the problem to the Problem Solver.

August 29

You Are Not A Slave to Fear

I prayed to the LORD, and he answered me. He freed me from all my fears. Psalm 34:4 NLT

There's an acronym for fear: F: false E: emotion A: appearing R: real. In other words, many of our fears may seem like they are real, but it's false. Fear can disrupt a lot of things in our lives. Fear can be displayed as not being enough, not being qualified in our place of assignment, or fear of the future. Many nurses also struggle with depression and rejection, which can lead to fear. We may find ourselves in situations that we never imagine. Even at that, fear is not a spirit that should be entertained in any way. Perhaps we want to exercise our faith by laying our hands on the sick, but fear will stop us from doing so because we do not want to be judged by unbelievers.

Christ has died for us, and He took away our fears. It's time to arise and take charge.

August 30

Peaceful Sleep

You can go to bed without fear; you will lie down and sleep soundly. Proverbs 3:24 NLT

The health care facility is a place where so many issues are treated; everyone is coming with different emotional, physical, mental, and spiritual issues. These people need help. The night is one of the deadliest times of the day, as some of these patients battle with their sleep. They lose their peace as they go through anguish and pains. Some are troubled with worries preventing them from sleeping. Some are going through demonic oppression and the captivity of the enemy. God has positioned us to be there for a purpose. We should use our authority as believers. This is beyond handling confrontational physical issues but also spiritual matters. When we take authority, we remind principalities and powers they have no space in our territory, and they will flee. We will see the peace of God move like never before. The Lord will also restore peace at night, and the patients will receive their healing.

Need for Rest

Even youths will become weak and tired, and young men will fall in exhaustion. But those who trust in the LORD will find new strength. They will soar high on wings like eagles. They will run and not grow weary. They will walk and not faint.
Isaiah 40:30-31 NLT

Relaxing is vital for optimal psychological and physiological functioning. There is a need to incorporate rest in our busy schedule. We should pay attention to our bodies as much as we do for the patients. Getting enough rest can help improve our productivity. It often requires that we move things and people around, which can take a toll on our physical energy. Sometimes we can have back pains from lifting heavy objects. Nurses are expected to be physically fit, mentally stable, and emotionally balanced to achieve peak performances. Regardless of how we want to listen to our bodies and take our personal routine, we should also look up to God to give us rest. He will reach out to us and fill us with His power and strength and give us the rest that we need.

September Health Awareness

Blood Cancer Awareness

Childhood Cancer Awareness

Ovarian Cancer Awareness

Polycystic Ovary Syndrome Month

Prostate Cancer Awareness

National Suicide Prevention Day (September 10)

September 1

God's Love Lasts Forever

*Love is patient and kind. Love is not jealous or boastful or proud
or rude. It does not demand its own way. It is not irritable, and it
keeps no record of being wronged. It does not rejoice about
injustice but rejoices whenever the truth wins out. Love never gives
up, never loses faith, is always hopeful, and endures through every
circumstance. Prophecy and speaking in unknown languages and
special knowledge will become useless. But love will last forever!*
1 Corinthians 13:4-8 NLT

When we experience true in our lives, we understand the importance of
loving others. There are those we may encounter who will make it
challenging to love them, but we must love them anyway. God commands
us to love, and if we love him, we must obey his commandments. You may
face a situation with a difficult co-worker or family member, but you must
still display God's love in your interactions with them. God desires for us to
be a living example of his love. God showed us the greatest example of how
much he loves us through the crucifixion of his son Jesus. Ask God to help
you today to love your enemy as you love yourself.

September 2

Trusting God

Trust in the Lord with all your heart and lean not on your own understanding. In all your ways submit to Him, and He will make your paths straight. Proverbs 3:5-6 NIV

When everything in our life seems to be going wrong, we must trust God's plan for us. We must not focus on our own thoughts, strategies, or ideas for the situation. God knows all that we encounter here on earth. God is aware of those things we experience, and He promises that we won't have to face them alone. To fully trust God, we must have faith that He will bring us through every situation, without exception. There are things in our lives that throw us off course, but God will come through for us. It's in those moments of uncertainty, we must rely on our faith to carry us through. Trust that God loves us and that He will never leave or forsake us. God shows us through multiple experiences that we can rely on Him entirely. Relying on God means trusting Him to take care of us in any situation. God wants us to believe in Him and to submit to Him in every area of our lives.

Gifts in The Body of Christ

For just as each of us has one body with many members, and these members do not all have the same function, so in Christ, we, though many, form one body, and each member belongs to all the others. Romans 12:4-5 NIV

In Romans 12, Paul makes an emotional appeal that we present our bodies as living sacrifices. We must totally and completely submit to God, not only when it is convenient to do so. Each day we must ask the Holy Spirit to take control of our thoughts and remain focused on God. Paul expressed how mature Christians should live, how we should work together in unity as one body in Christ. Each of us must realize that we have spiritual gifts, and we each bring value to the body of Christ. While we are unique, in our own uniqueness, we have the same purpose, which is to win souls for Christ. There are many gifts in the body of Christ, and it is vital to know who we are and what we do well. We must remain faithful and serve others with that which Christ has provided us. Titles do not define who we are in God; therefore, we cannot become caught up in how people define us. Once we remind ourselves that we are all in this together to advance the Kingdom, we are better able to operate in our gifts. The basic concept is the same in our workplaces as we each bring different strengths to our teams. Be wise not to overlook the introverts. Introverts have just as much to offer as the extrovert.

Peace Be Still

And the peace of God which transcends all understanding
will guard your hearts and your minds in Christ Jesus.
Philippians 4:7 NIV

There are times when circumstances cause us to feel as if things are spinning out of control. We each face difficult situations or storms in our lives at one time or another. God reminds us in his word that He will keep in perfect peace all who trust in Him, and all whose thoughts are fixed on Him.

We have an assurance that whatever we encounter, God is with us. In those challenging moments, we must cling to God's word and trust that He will provide the peace that he promises; the peace that surpasses understanding.

Psalm 46 says, Be still and know that I am God! I will be honored by every nation; I will be honored throughout the world. This reminds us that nothing can happen in our lives that God does not allow. We must be still and know that He is God. God will cause every storm or situation to cease. He is quite capable of handling anything we face. Today, when you find yourself worrying about how you will make it through the day, say to yourself, "Peace be still" and watch God work on your behalf.

September 5

God Is in Control

But blessed are those who trust in the Lord and have made the Lord their hope and confidence. They are like trees planted along a riverbank, with roots that reach deep into the water. Such trees are not bothered by the heat or worried by long months of drought. Their leaves stay green, and they never stop producing fruit.
Jeremiah 17:7-8 NLT

Many of us have been trying to make sense of our experiences during the different seasons of our lives. God's word reminds us to trust in the Lord with all our hearts, believing he is able and wise to do what is best. Some may experience anxiety, fear, doubt, and even anger with others and with God concerning the loss and sickness of loved ones. Some of these feelings are a result of us leaning on our own understanding. Often, when we journey through these seasons, we desire to take control, but God's word tells us to trust Him. We won't understand some things, and there are some things that God will reveal to us, but we can't rely on our wisdom. God grants us godly wisdom as it relates to our daily decision, but our ultimate trust and understanding must be fixed on Him. We must pray that even during these times that we would trust God to simply be God.

September 6

Larger Than Legos

Woe to the world because of its stumbling blocks! For it is inevitable that stumbling blocks come; but Woe to that man through whom the stumbling block comes! Matthew 18:7 NIV

The Bible warns us as Christians that we will come upon situations that will cause us to stumble, it calls them stumbling blocks, and now more than ever, it seems as though the world is full of them. Stumbling blocks are those things that can derail us from our walk with God and distract us from our purpose or from adopting the heart and character of God in that given moment.

They may be secret addictions, gossiping, tempers and deportment. They are varied from person to person. So how then does the Bible treat stumbling blocks? It instructs us as believers to be sure that our conduct reflects God at all times. This is no small order in the current emotionally charged world we live in. The temptation to give in to our most natural impulses is always at the forefront of our minds as people, but they should be filtered through Christ as his followers.

If we consciously act contrary to God's nature and misrepresent Him in our conduct, we will have to give an account for this. We are encouraged to glean strength to stand against evil with God as our general, our example and our muse.

Nothing Between

You shall have no other gods before Me. Exodus 20:3 NIV

What is it that is standing between you and God? Is it perhaps a busy schedule? Elderly parents? A demanding job? Noisy children? Exhaustion? What are the excuses that we use to justify our failure to spend time with God?

There should be nothing that stands in the way of us spending quality time with God. Don't worry, I'm not judging you. As a matter of fact, we are all guilty of getting so busy at times that we forget to pray. God called us to live lives of temperance. He asks us to do everything in moderation. Sure, He expects us to have different elements in our lives. There is nothing wrong with having a packed schedule, but in your schedule, have you made time for God? If not, then your schedule is standing between your soul and your Savior. You have to ask yourself which one is more important. When you wake up in the morning, is God the first person that you speak with? Is your response to the gift of life, gratitude for each new day, or do you automatically check your emails or timeline to see what you've missed? Do you pause to give thanks for the borrowed breath that you breathe each day? If not, I encourage you to start today. There are many important things in our lives, but all things that we have come from God. It is, therefore, important that we keep the channel clear and make sure that there is nothing that we have put in His place.

September 8

Godly Community

Let us consider one another to stir up love and good works, not forsaking the assembling of ourselves together, as is the manner of some, but exhorting one another, and so much the more as you see the Day approaching. Hebrews 10:24-25 NKJV

The Christian walk is not meant to be lonely. God is a God of community. We see this in him surrounding himself with 12 other men on the same mission as he was during his brief time on earth. This is important, as the word says that iron sharpens iron.

It is easy to become distracted by our own problems and forget the many times that God has come through for us, but if we surround ourselves with people who share our love for God and a desire to grow as believers and to do the will of God, then we find that we will be held accountable. We discover that we will be encouraged and strengthened in our faith, and these kinds of friendships are the friendships that feed our souls. They are the friendships that we can turn to and depend on when things go wrong. We are reminded in the word to not forsake the fellowship of believers because he knew just how important it is for us to share our lives with others. In the same way that we should share the Word of God, we should also share ourselves with our community, our physical community, and our church community so that others may be strengthened by our experiences and draw strength from the experiences of others.

September 9

The B.I.B.L.E

All scripture is given by inspiration of God, and is profitable for doctrine, for reproof, for correction, for instruction in righteousness: That the man of God may be perfect, thoroughly furnished unto all good works. 2 Timothy 3:16-17 KJV

Skeptics have questioned the validity and importance of the Bible for years. We have seen and heard various theories surrounding the authorship of the Word of God. We've even heard accusations hurled against the Word of God.

So, how important is the Bible to modern Christianity? It is very relevant. The Bible is still God's way of communicating with us in writing. It has been passed down for years and is profitable for doctrine and reproof. Without the Word of God, human beings would forget not just all that God has already done, but who God is.

While he makes himself manifest to us in different ways, generations without the word would live in misery because they are disconnected from the source of their joy. The Bible is a lamp post. It is a source of peace and sound correction. The Bible is still as relevant today as it was in the past and even more so now. It helps us to understand the times in which we live and to find comfort in knowing that God, in His love for us, warned us of all these things that were to come. It shows us the way out of our situations and guides us into the land of peace.

September 10

Patience

But you, O man of God, flee these things and pursue
righteousness, godliness, faith, love, patience, gentleness.
1 Timothy 6:11 NKJV

We live in a very fast-paced, get it now, get it done kind of world. Patience is seen as being merely a virtue, which it might be, but real patience comes from God. We know that the trying of our faith brings patience, and we also know that anything that is aligned with our faith is of great importance.

Why is patience such a big deal? Without patience, we may trick ourselves into thinking that we are the masters of our own destiny. Without patience, we forget what it is like to submit ourselves to prayer and fasting. We expect God to act within our time, and we complain when He does not. Patience comes with faith because God sometimes allows us to wait on Him, and His time is not our time. He sees the end, He sees the beginning, He knows all things, and He does not need to answer to us, but he does answer us. There's a big difference.

If we remain patient, when we pray, we will hear the answers. It may not always be the answer that we want, but it is an answer nonetheless, and if we are patient, we will see the wisdom of God made manifest in the changed circumstances that are sure to come from acting according to his will.

September 11

Where Is Your Heart?

Search me, God, and know my heart; test me and know my anxious thoughts. See if there is any offensive way in me, and lead me in the way everlasting. Psalm 139:23-24 NIV

Who do you really serve?

This is decided by the "location of your heart. I once heard that to determine the love of your life, you should visit your bank account. This is because, as the Bible says, where your treasure is, your heart will also be. How diligent are we in giving to God what is rightfully His? How do we feel about giving back to others in service to God? How do you feel about donating to causes, or merely being a good neighbor? Is there anything that God is not allowed to touch?

Is your heart fixed on heaven? These are the kind of questions that we should be asking ourselves as believers daily. We should never become so comfortable in our title of "Christian" that we forget what it means to actually be a Christian (a follower and representative of Christ). We should always remember what we are called to do. We should check ourselves regularly to ensure that we are not missing the mark because it is possible to be in God's presence every day just like Judas was, and still be lost. Judas should have asked himself some serious questions, and because he did not, he did not realize the true nature of his own heart.

We should not allow ourselves to fall into the same trap that he did. Examine yourselves daily. Examine your heart and your relationship with God and find ways to deepen that connection, because, at the end of the day, it is the only thing that matters.

September 12

What is love?

Again Jesus said, "Simon son of John, do you love me?" He answered, "Yes, Lord, you know that I love you." Jesus said, "Take care of my sheep." John 21:16 NIV

If you are a Christian, then I'm quite sure that when asked if you love Jesus, you would say yes, but what does it really mean to love the Lord? How do we demonstrate our love for God? How are we required to express our love for God? Do they align?

Is it enough to attending services or giving spare change to the poor and offer quick words of prayer as we rush through the door or before we pass out for the night?

Is loving God done by publicly stating that we are Christians? Are those really acts of love, or do we see our love for God as yet another fleeting feeling that we can compare to emotional experiences when in the presence of other people? Our love for God should be deeper than that. Our love for God should be made manifest in every area of our life. It should be demonstrated in the way we eat, drink, and speak as well as in the things we think about. Our love for God should be so strong that it remains relevant when there is no one else around. It should be the foundation of who we are and not merely another thing that we do, feel, or experience. Our love for God should be the cornerstone of our lives and the reference point of who we are. It should not be dependent on our words or environment; it should not be dependent on where we are at the time and who we are with. Our love for God should be based on the infinite and unchanging nature of God because his love for us is as firm and unchanging as He is.

September 13

Back to the Basics

I will praise thee with my whole heart: before the gods will I sing praise unto thee. Psalm 138:1 KJV

When was the last time you stopped to count your blessings? When was the last time you saw adversity as an opportunity to give praise? If you don't make it a habit, perhaps you should revisit Paul's life. Brother Paul spent most of his ministry in captivity or suffering at the hands of others for the sake of the gospel, and yet, if asked to count his blessings, Paul would give you a list as long as you can imagine. He could praise in every moment because he saw every opportunity as a gift from God. Paul saw persecution as a means to an end. He saw imprisonment as another opportunity to share God's goodness because he focused on God and not on his problems. We are encouraged to do the very same thing. We are encouraged to store the Word of God in our hearts so that when we are put in situations that we would rather not be in; we can count our blessings.

September 14

The Secret to Seeing God

The earth is the Lord's, and the fullness thereof; the world, and they that dwell therein. Psalm 24:1 KJV

If you listen to the birds in the early morning anywhere between 4 & 5 a.m., you can hear them chirping loudly, singing amidst the silence, and it's as if there is a symphony of praise happening right outside your door. Human beings are the most complicated creatures that God made. If we observe nature, we see the simplicity of the praise that God expects of us. Every morning, when the birds rise from their sleep, they proceed to sing praises to the Lord. It may be noisy for us, but I'm quite sure it's music to God's ears. This is what the Lord wants. He wants us to see him in all things. God wants us to see our problems and tell them about God. He wants us to look at nature and see him. He wants us to look into ourselves, and desire to be like him. God wants to be the center of our universe because He is the center of the world. The earth is the Lord's and the fullness thereof, yet he will never force us into a relationship with Him.

Kingdom Quest

But seek ye first the kingdom of God and his righteousness, and all these things shall be added unto you. Matthew 6:33 KJV

What is it that we are working to gain? What is our ultimate purpose here on earth? Have we forgotten our calling as Christians? Have we allowed the demands of our jobs and our extracurricular activities to distract us from the reality that our time here on earth is not permanent and that this is not our final home?

We are warned repeatedly not to conform to the world. We are told to store up our treasures in heaven. This is not to say that we should not pursue things while here on earth, but we are encouraged in the Word of God to seek God's kingdom before all else. If our pursuits are empty of God, then they are still useless. It does not matter how successful we are in any area; success without God is meaningless. Are you striving towards earthly goals, or are you still, as a believer, waiting with expectation in your heart and with a song on your lips, for the second coming of our Lord?

September 16

Find Your Footing

And David spoke to the men that stood by him, saying, what shall be done to the man that killeth this Philistine, and taketh away the reproach from Israel? For who is this uncircumcised Philistine, that he should defy the armies of the living God? 1 Samuel 17:26 KJV

We live in a very diverse world. We live in a world where religious liberty is protected by law. However, while we remain respectful of others, we must also stand up for our God. God does not need us to defend Him. He does not need us to protect him either, but by defending our faith, we strengthen our faith.

When we speak out when others are speaking against God instead of nervously doubting God, we remind ourselves of who God is to us. When we hear ourselves talk about the goodness and the awesomeness of God, without getting into altercations that lead to sinfulness and sinful interactions, we glorify God. Our primary purpose on earth is to be loyal to God, and so whenever we are in a space where God's character is being called into question, it is our duty as Christians to speak up about the goodness of God and to do so in a way that brings him glory.

September 17

Quality Time

Thou wilt keep him in perfect peace, whose mind is stayed on thee: because he trusteth in thee. Isaiah 26:3 KJV

There is just something special about our time alone with God. There is something powerful about getting quiet and dwelling in the presence of an Almighty God who knows all things, controls everything, and is concerned about our well-being. It is essential that we set aside time every day to have devotion with the Lord. When we check through Bible history, we see all the major and minor prophets waking up early to spend time with the Lord; to spend quiet time in his presence. The combination of silence and praise is seemingly the perfect environment within which to visit with God. We can hear him clearly when our minds are fixed and focused on Him. When our hearts are in tune and aligned with his presence, we are not distracted by everything that is happening around us.

September 18

Our Hope

And his disciples came to him, and awoke him, saying, Lord, save us: we perish. And he saith unto them, Why are ye fearful, O ye of little faith? Then he arose and rebuked the winds and the sea, and there was a great calm. But the men marveled, saying, What manner of man is this, that even the winds and the sea obey him!
Matthew 8:25-27 KJV

It almost seems ridiculous to talk about hope, joy, and peace in times of crisis. It seems virtually insensitive as though we're trying and downplay the severity of the situation that is currently taking place around us. However, the Christian's hope is not insensitive. It is a hope that is in place all year round and is not affected by any crisis. It is peace amid storms.

We have a God who is much bigger than every situation that we could ever experience. We have a God who is capable of reaching down and pulling us out of darkness, and because of this, we should not walk like those who have no hope. We should walk in assurance and share our hope with those looking for something to fill the God-sized hole in their life so that they, too, can experience peace during their storm.

Compassion

Carry each other's burdens, and in this way you will fulfill the law of Christ. Galatians 6:2 NIV

Death is as unfortunate as it is inevitable. This is real to us as nurses who have to deal with the realities of the temporary nature of man almost daily. Dealing with patients who eventually pass away has undoubtedly affected all of us. We watch families mourn their loved ones, and we mourn patients who have bonded over time. We watch as people experience the pain of loss, and we try to provide comfort, sometimes putting ourselves directly in the line of fire. In emotionally charged situations, it is easy to take things personally. When persons respond to us from pain and anger, our responsibility in moments of grief is to provide comfort. This is our duty not just as nurses but as Christians. We provide support to those who may feel alone, and in doing so, we reflect the heart of a God who is moved by death and loss. God understands the pain that we feel, and he wants us to be there for each other when these inevitabilities happen. The Lord blesses those who mourn because they will be comforted in the end, but while they are here, we must ensure that we provide comfort not just to our patients but also to everyone we come in contact with. When we look around, we see many opportunities to offer support. We see families that have been broken into pieces, devastated by unemployment, poverty, and other crises that are quickly becoming commonplace in our society. It is our duty as Christians to bring the message of hope into a dark world.

September 20

Christ's Body

What? Know ye not that your body is the temple of the Holy Ghost which is in you, which ye have of God, and ye are not your own?
1 Corinthians 6:19 KJV

Being busy has become the norm in our society. For many of us, the busier we are, the more productive we feel. Whether or not this is actually true, in the hustle and bustle of everyday life, we often neglect our own health. In trying to care for everyone else, we are prone to missing meals and other harmful habits that eventually have adverse effects on our bodies. It is essential, especially to us as believers, that we remember that our bodies are the temple of Christ, and while God is represented in our work and made manifest by our service, He wants to be glorified in all that we do. So, the way that we treat our bodies is also important to him. It is not enough to take care of everyone else if the temple that we have been blessed with is not kept in optimal health.

September 21

No Worries

Don't be afraid, for I am with you. Don't be discouraged, for I am your God. I will strengthen you and help you. I will hold you up with my victorious right hand. Isaiah 41:10 NLT

As far as essential services and servanthood goes, nurses have always been essential to society. Around the world, nurses are treated with varying degrees of respect and receive universally inadequate compensation for all that they do. In the time we live; however, there is no question about the importance of the work we do. All health fraternity and medical industry members have been labeled as heroes as we combat one critical virus after another. It is easy to become anxious in the face of all these new diseases while we pledged our service to the betterment of society. We are still people. However, as believers in Christ, we are called to live a life not just of service but a life free from anxiety and worry. We are encouraged to be watchful, diligent, and humble, but we are also encouraged to keep our faith strong, to keep your eyes on the Lord, and too plant our hope in God.

September 22

Thy Will Be Done

After this manner, therefore, pray ye: Our Father which art in heaven, Hallowed be thy name. Thy kingdom come, Thy will be done in earth, as it is in heaven. Matthew 6:9,10 KJV

We are taught to pray in faith and with high expectations. We are told that whatsoever we ask in the name of Jesus will be given to us, and so we storm heaven with audacious prayers and pour out the desires of our hearts. When Jesus taught the disciples how to pray, he revealed the importance of acknowledging that regardless of what we ask for and what we want, God's response will be in accordance with God's will.

"They will be done on earth as it is in heaven" shows us that God's will rules over the entire universe. When we pray, it is equally important that we acknowledge that our desires should fall under God's will.

When Mary and Martha sent for Jesus, they expected him to show up. They expected him to come into their situation and heal it as they had seen him do before. Their will was based on the limited view they had of Jesus, but Jesus had a different plan.

The siblings did nothing wrong. They were not disrespectful in their request, and they were sincere in their faith, so why was Lazarus allowed to die? Because their request was not in accordance with God's will. They wanted healing, but Jesus wanted a resurrection.

When we pray and ask that God's will be done, we leave room for him to surprise us with a miracle of his own design.

September 23

Vacation Denied

Therefore, since we are surrounded by such a great cloud of witnesses, let us throw off everything that hinders and the sin that so easily entangles. And let us run with perseverance the race marked out for us. Hebrews 12:1 NIV

We all look forward to taking long breaks where we can relax with our friends, family, or catch up on some well-deserved sleep. We love the idea of not having an alarm go off to wake us up and not having to stick to the same old routine as we've always done. Vacation days are everything!

In our Christian walk, however, we don't get to take days off or call in sick. We have to show up every day, robed in the armor of God, ready to go out into a world of sin and be set apart. When we decide to take a break from being saints, we fall into serious trouble. We leave ourselves wide open to multiple attacks from the enemy, and we may even start to lose faith.

When we look to the bible, we see examples of men like Jonah, David, and even Elijah, who applied for vacation days. Jonah just wasn't having the work schedule that God placed on the roster, David decided to play hooky, and Elijah mentally checked out for a quick second after being threatened by a savage Queen.

In each of these instances, the response from management was the same: vacation denied. Look at the consequences of taking a break from being obedient and standing boldly in God's word and decide today that you want stamina to finish the entire race.

September 24

Guilty Pleasures

If we confess our sins, he is faithful and just to forgive us our sins and to cleanse us from all unrighteousness. 1 John 1:9 KJV

We all have weaknesses. Some of us are more patient than others, some of us are less calm than others, and even more of us struggle with the principle of forgiveness. If the Christian's life were to be summarized by a sign, it would most likely read "Work in Progress."

God knows this about us. He knows that we are not perfect and that we need grace every day. He is willing to supply His grace and to forgive our sins, but before He can do that, there is something that we need to do.

Have you ever seen a child try to lie about stealing candy, ice cream, or cookies? Any treat that leaves a residue as evidence that this child who insists on his or her innocence, is not telling the truth.

As adults, it is obvious to us that they're lying, but they're convinced that they're doing a great job at pulling the wool over your eyes, so they keep going. To them, they have this well-kept secret, but to us, all we can see are the chocolate marks, the cookie crumbs, and the ice cream stains.

It is the same way with us. We are quick to confess the "big" sins that we despise, but we lie to ourselves about our guilty pleasures. We get a rush from telling someone off, or we feel vindicated when we take matters into our own hands, or perhaps we struggle with sexual sins or unforgiveness; it doesn't matter. When we try to downplay the seriousness of the problem and not bring it to God, he can see the evidence of the stains of sin all over our lives. He knows we're lying to ourselves, and we're lying to Him. He encourages us to walk away from all sin. There are no exceptions.

Word Wars

Pleasant words are as a honeycomb, sweet to the soul, and health to the bones. Proverbs 16:24 KJV

We have long past the stage where we believe that words do not carry weight. This has been proven to be false, as words can be more damaging than physical blows. With our words, we can encourage and inspire others to bring them closer to God, or we can drive them away from him, spread lies about his character, and ultimately destroy someone else's desire to connect with God.

We are cautioned to choose our words carefully, to speak words that are flowing from the heart of God, to prayerfully pick our words, and to not just throw them around.

As Christians, our words will expose us because the bible says that out of the abundance of the heart, the mouth will speak. If our words are faulty, then it points to faulty hearts, and if our words are seasoned with grace consistently, then it speaks to a heart that bows in the presence of the Lord.

September 26

What Does God Say?

But ye are a chosen generation, a royal priesthood, a holy nation,
a peculiar people; that ye should shew forth the praises of him
who hath called you out of darkness into his marvelous light.
1 Peter 2:9 KJV

It can sometimes be challenging to not internalize the negative things that were perhaps said about us growing up. We may have heard somethings that we knew were wrong, even if we didn't quite understand what was wrong about them. Over time, however, as the years passed, these words became more familiar, and eventually, for some of us, we stopped questioning them. We accepted them as being a part of who we are; words like; lazy, ugly, worthless, stupid, and destined for failure. Subconsciously, we allowed these negative things to seep into our identity, and as we grew older, it became difficult to get rid of them.

The problem with this is that every negative thing that the devil would have you believe about yourself goes against everything that God said about us. Yes, we flawed sinners in need of God. When we walk with the Lord, we are called chosen, special, set apart, fearfully and wonderfully made, blessed, and highly favored. None of these things are ever said to us by the devil because he wants you to believe that you are useless. He wants you to believe all the negative things because maybe you will never achieve the potential that God put in your heart. If you don't think that you deserve a seat at the table, you never try to get a foot into the door. Today, I want to encourage you to read deeply into the word and find out what God says is possible through His power. Read and uncover the nature of God's mercy and how it can transform the lives of men.

The Challenge

In your anger, do not sin." Do not let the sun go down while you are still angry. Ephesians 4:26 NIV

As a community, we are not short on reasons to get angry. We are not short on justifiable rage. As human beings, we get upset whenever our expectations go unmet, if our egos are wounded if we fail at something because it's blocked unjustly, if feelings get hurt or if there's any kind of injustice. Ephesians tells us that even in our anger, we should not sin. This is no small feat.

The Bible gives us permission to be angry, but we also have to be aware that God does not give us a license to sin. Anger is an appropriate response to a perversion of justice, crime, an attack on our family, or a personal attack. God is seen in the word as being angry at things, but unlike us, God's anger never erupts into something that can damage his relationship with his people. God's wrath is channeled in the same way that ours should be directed. Meaningless anger gets us nowhere. It's a feeling that consumes us, an emotion that overwhelms and exhausts us, but it does not affect change by itself. Anger is not a sin, but unforgiveness is. Psalm 37:8 says, stop being angry, turn from your rage, do not lose your temper; it only leads to harm.

God wants what is best for us in every situation, and there are no exceptions to this rule. God loves all of us, and he sees us hurting each other, which makes him angry, yet he extends grace and mercy. At the same time, he executes consequences. Forgiveness is not the absence of consequences; mercy is.

September 28

Run for Cover

God is our refuge and strength, a very present help in trouble.
Psalm 46:1 KJV

Have you ever found yourself outside at the moment when the rain is about to start pouring down? You look to your left and right, but there are no buildings in sight; bus station, ledges, or awnings. All you can see is a clear path ahead of you, storm clouds over you, and no umbrella in sight. What do you do?

If you're anything like me, you start walking really quickly. your aim is to get to the point where you can get shelter and not be caught in the rain. The same thing is real in the spiritual sense. When we look to the left, and we look to the right of us in this world, all we can see is darkness. All we can see are broken people with broken feelings and lost looks behind their eyes. We want to run away from the tribulation and negativity, and the only place where we can find shelter is in God, who promises to be a refuge or shelter in the storm. God has promised us that he will always shield us and protect us. It is for us to claim his promises to claim his words as being true and to sprint to him so that we can be protected when the storm hits.

Money Matters

Lazy people are soon poor; hard workers get rich.
Proverbs 10:4 NLT

Have you ever tried going to the supermarkets and paying for your goods with a smile, a hug, a kind word, or a good gesture? If you have, then you would have figured out what the rest of us already knew, that those things, while extremely valuable and while meaningful, don't necessarily act as the proper currency in every situation.

As Christians, we sometimes grapple with the idea of valuing money because many of us were told growing up that money is the root of all evil. The reality is that the Bible never said that. The Bible never said that money was evil. It never said that money was the root of evil, it said that the love of money was.

When the Bible uses the word love, it hardly ever has the transient, flimsy definition that we tend to use as people. When you love something, it takes over your life. It consumes all that you are, and so when you love money, you will do anything for it. You are willing to compromise values that you thought were etched in stone to achieve a particular purpose, but never mind that that purpose may not be within God's will.

In the same breath, God does not endorse laziness or unambitious. God would have it that we pursue our purpose with a sense of excellence about us, and if we're going to be paid for it, we do our work to the highest standard possible so that we may be justly rewarded. Do not fall into the trap of providing substandard work because your aim is "not to amass wealth." Substandard work does not glorify God because God does not do anything halfway.

Whatever God does is done well, and we should seek to be more like him.

September 30

I Am

And God said unto Moses, I Am That I Am: and he said, Thus shalt thou say unto the children of Israel, I Am hath sent me unto you. Exodus 3:14 KJV

We will never fully understand the fullness of God. He is bigger than our imagination, and more powerful than our minds can fathom. Yet, this big God is willing to hear us when we cry out to him, to fight battles on our behalf, and to watch over us daily. There is nothing that we can throw at God that can overwhelm Him. Do you need comfort? He is the comforter. Do you need healing? He is the mighty healer. Do you need food, money, or a job? He is Jehovah Jireh, your provider. Ask him in earnest according to his will to pour out blessings in your life, to give you wisdom, and to keep you in perfect peace.

God is not limited by our inability to comprehend him, and he is not restricted to our thoughts. There is no explaining away the nature of God, he simply is. When asked about his name, God's response was very simple yet incredibly profound.

He said, "I am that I am," and He left it there. Who He is would fill the pages of the world because He is everything to everyone who needs Him? He is Father, King, Doctor, and friend. We have done nothing to deserve this love and can do nothing to deserve it, but we can seek daily to bask in His presence and deepen our love for Him as we prepare for His return.

October Health Awareness

Domestic Violence Awareness

Health Literacy Month

National Breast Cancer Awareness

National Bullying Prevention

National Down's Syndrome

SIDS Awareness

October 1

Unlocking God's Password

Worship the LORD with gladness. Come before him, singing with joy. Psalm 100:2 NLT

A password consists of a secret word or phrase that is unique to the user and must be used to gain admission to a place, such as bank account or an internet website. As believers, we can gain access to God's heart by worshipping and praising Him wholeheartedly on a daily basis. When we go through difficult times in our personal life, instead of complaining about the things we lack, we should change our confession into thanksgiving. Let us remain thankful for everything and complain about nothing. I thank God that everything is working together for my good. We should endeavor to make it a habit to enter God's password every day with thanksgiving. Don't listen to the lies of the devil. Unlock the heart of God with your password of thanks. Even if what you are trusting God for has not been delivered to you, still thank Him.

October 2

Pray with Specificity

When you pray, don't babble on and on as people of other religions do. They think their prayers are answered merely by repeating their words again and again. Don't be like them, for your Father knows exactly what you need even before you ask him! Matthew 6:7-8 NLT

God deals with details and specificity. We are reminded about the story of Noah in the Bible; we read how God gave him specific measurements for building the ark. In the same way, God needs us to ask Him exactly what we want; you have a blank cheque, so fill it up by faith. If there's anything we need, and we are bold enough to ask God By faith, we will surely receive them according to His timing. We need to stop praying vague prayers and become specific not only in our line of profession but also in our personal lives. We say vague prayers and get disappointed when nothing we have asked for is answered in the way that we want. We are encouraged to start praying with specificity.

October 3

We Are the Image of God

So God created human beings in his own image. In the image of God he created them; male and female he created them. Genesis 1:27 NLT

We serve a great God that took His time to create us; He breathes life and greatness into us. We are not living for the accolades of men but the purpose of God. You are not a biological accident; do not listen to the lies of the devil. Imagine how great your God is, imagine all the great people in the Bible; you are also one of them. God is going to use you mightily in this generation. God will use you to heal the sick and raise the dead. Don't ever feel inferior because of your financial status, social status, marital status, or because your mates have gone ahead of you. We are not running a physical race with anybody; our only race is to make heaven. Take care of yourself. Believe in yourself. Be happy. Rejoice in the Lord. Pamper yourself. Love yourself and call yourself what God calls you.

October 4

Being the Vessel for God's Vision

Then the LORD said to me, "Write my answer plainly on tablets, so that a runner can carry the correct message to others.
Habakkuk 2:2 NLT

God is looking for vessels and voices to use to carry out His vision. God's vision is not your ambition. His vision is what He wants to make out of your life, and that will disrupt your own agenda and ambition. It should be our honor and blessing to others when we walk in God's vision for our lives. The best part of it is to finish well, as our role models in the Bible. We should carry out God's vision of our place of assignment. We cannot miss our destiny when we align with God's vision.

October 5

The Desert Will Bloom

I will not die; instead, I will live to tell what the LORD has done.
Psalm 118:17 NLT

The dictionary definition of the word "desert" is a barren place, ill-suited for life. Viewed from this angle, the desert is not very appealing. And yet, God's creation is full of beautiful surprises and rich with teachings. Maybe, we are going through the dry, scorching wind of the desert right now? If so, what is the desert called? Depression… Divorce… Sickness… Loneliness… Something else…? Whatever its name, this dessert will not be our tomb. We will not be buried in it. We will not die in the desert... we will live. Yes, we will live and declare the works of the Lord!

October 6

When It Is Beyond Your Ability

He gives power to the weak and strength to the powerless.
Isaiah 40:29 NLT

As wise and confident as we may be, some situations are beyond us. Have you acknowledged recently that you've reached the end of your limits? We should rely completely on God when we can't do everything. No one is a Superman or Superwoman. We should make use of HIS solution. For instance, when you realize that after praying for a sick patient, they keep getting worse, keep trusting God. With the Holy Spirits guide, we will no longer rely on our own strengths, but solely totally trust in God.

October 7

You Are Built for This

The LORD supports the humble, but he brings the wicked down into the dust. Psalm 147:6 NLT

As Christians, our lives are not always about victories and easy times. However, we are equipped to stand firm, even through adversities. Our attitude in difficult moments will spread to those all around us. God created us for a purpose. For every challenge we go through, He has empowered us to overcome them. We are built to help humanity and restore their spirituality as Christians. We should be the reason the sick, and dying patients still have confidence in God, especially for their healing.

October 8

Hearing God's Voice

My sheep listen to my voice; I know them, and they follow me.
John 10:27 NLT

God's voice is a heavenly or divine voice that proclaims His will or judgment. The prophets in the Old Testament heard God's voice, but today, Jesus has sent us the Holy Spirit to help us hear and discern His voice. We can go through life with ease and walk in the vision and will of God by daily hearing from Him. For instance, when someone close to us speaks from a distance, we can decipher because we are familiar with the voice. We can hear the voice of God through studying the Bible daily, praying daily, renewing our mind with the messages of God daily, seeking to know God more, and praying in the Holy Ghost. God is daily speaking to us regarding our lives, businesses, careers, relationships, marriage, finances, opportunities, health, families, bad habits, friends to connect with, friends to disconnect from, where to go and where not to go. How often do we hear God's voice?

October 9

Jesus Is the Great Physician

Jesus said, "I will come and heal him." Matthew 8:7 NLT

We encounter situations that leave us devastated, perhaps standing in the place of prayer for a patient whose health is deteriorating. We need to introduce Jesus as the great physician to them. We need to make them understand that the medication is just human methodology. Jesus is the only One that heals divinely, and there will be total restoration. We are only trying our best as medical practitioners, but God is the only One that heals. When we go about telling them this, reassuring the healing power of God to them, we are thereby helping them to build faith and truly reminding God to take over the situation.

Dealing with An Unbeliever

God sent his Son into the world not to judge the world, but to save the world through him. John 3:17 NLT

We are called to be ambassadors of Christ, to preach the gospel to as many people that we encounter. It may come easily when we are preaching to believers who have similar values and faith. However, when we encounter unbelievers or people of a different faith, it can be a little more difficult, especially in hospitals. These patients are in dire need of a miracle, and telling them about Jesus Whom they probably haven't heard about may be very confusing for them. In this situation, we need to let the Holy Spirit lead us on the right things to say. Whether or not they accept Jesus shouldn't be our concern, our concern should be to preach the Word and let the Holy Spirit do the work in them.

October 11

God Has the Final Say

My heart has heard you say, "Come and talk with me." And my heart responds, "LORD, I am coming." Psalm 27:8 NLT

There are cases where the patients we are tending to have been given a diagnosis, and they have accepted their fate. This is the time, as believers, we come in to tell them that God has the final say. Let us raise instances of health issues in the Bible that Jesus healed. From the Old Testament to the New Testament, we have had cases of divine healing and God's perfect restoration. Abraham and Sarah believed God for a son; even at old age, God still changed their story. In today's world, we would call it impotence or fertility issues, but God changed the story. Let us remain patient and continually trust in God for the final say over our patients' health.

The Hem of Jesus' Garment

They begged him to let the sick touch at least the fringe of his robe, and all who touched him were healed. Matthew 14:36 NLT

The Bible tells us about the story of the woman with the issue of blood. This woman always looked out for Jesus, but the massive crowd wouldn't allow her to get to Jesus for her healing. She said to herself if only she could touch the hem of Jesus's garment, she would be healed. Eventually, she found her way to Jesus's garment, and she was healed. In the same way, we should encourage patients to touch the hem of Jesus' garment through prayers. Prayers can solve all kinds of problems. It is our weapon as Christians; therefore, as nurses, we encourage patients to be prayerful. We should as well be fervent in prayers.

October 13

The Need for Divine Equipment

Work hard so you can present yourself to God and receive his approval. Be a good worker, one who does not need to be ashamed and who correctly explains the word of truth. 2 Timothy 2:15 NLT

Working as a nurse requires us always to have our equipment at hand. We keep a stethoscope or and other medical equipment within our reach in cases of emergencies. This is exactly what we should do with our spiritual weapons. We need to surround ourselves with divine equipment to carry out our duties as believers daily. We need the Bible, a spiritual weapon to feed our minds and also that of our patients. 2 Timothy 2 tells us that we are to study to show ourselves approved because the enemy is daily at war with our minds. Therefore, carrying and using our divine equipment helps us to get the victory.

The Good Shepherd

The LORD is my shepherd; I have all that I need. Psalm 23:1 NLT

The psalmist called God the Good Shepherd in difficult times of need. God is always there. We are His sheep, and He will never abandon or forsake us. Have we been in positions where it seemed like we wanted to give up on a particular case, especially with a patient that was a believer? Do we sometimes feel we are wasting our time praying or trusting God for a miracle when it might be in our finance? Let us remember God is the Good Shepherd. He is constantly reaching out to us in innumerable ways. The fact that we can read this devotional today is enough reason to know that God is a good shepherd. He is reminding you of His love and mercy. God can never abandon His sheep.

October 15

You Are God's Asset

For we are both God's workers. And you are God's field. You are God's building. 1 Corinthians 3:9 NLT

Have you had any reason to second-guess yourself? Being a Christian doesn't even help the matter; we feel so inferior, especially when a colleague is being appreciated or appraised, leaving us unrecognized for the efforts we have made. We sometimes go above and beyond not just for the income but for the love of humanity, and as Christian, we stretch ourselves to do the work of God. We don't get enough recognition, applauds, compliments, or sometimes encouragement. God is saying to us today that we are His assets. As nurses, we are daily fulfilling His purpose, striving to honor Him at all times, and winning Souls to Him through our actions.

October 16

The Way, The Truth, And the Life

Jesus told him, "I am the way, the truth, and the life. No one can come to the Father except through me." John 14:6 NLT

It is not surprising to see people dying with the nature of our job. As a matter of fact, people die every day. The Bible tells us the devil has come to steal, kill, and destroy, but Jesus has come to give us life in abundance. We need to help our patients to give their lives to Christ before they take their last breath. In cases when a patient is about to die, they are usually very venerable. Help me to say or do something today that will glorify you.

October 17

The Giver of Life

For you are the fountain of life, the light by which we see.
Psalm 36:9 NLT

There was a beginning because God is already there. Our lives were pre-designed by the owner, and He made it the way He wanted. God gives us life for a reason, and that reason can only be found in His will. We are not here by accident. God breathes His life into us for His own purpose. When we are faced with trials and tribulations, we should always remember that this life isn't ours. God gave it to us, and we should also channel that energy into the way we communicate with the patients in our care—helping them to understand that God is the giver of life.

October 18

Be Kind to Yourself

No one hates his own body but feeds and cares for it, just as Christ cares for the church. Ephesians 5:29 NLT

The emotional, mental, and physical stress that the jobs bring can be overwhelming. We are taught as Christians to show kindness and empathy to our patients; however, oftentimes, we care so much about others we forget ourselves. This is very unhealthy as we might end up in the sickbed if we don't look after ourselves. It is essential that we have a life after the confines of our job. Hanging out with families, giving ourselves some special treat, eating well, and having enough rest can go a long way in our physical, mental, and emotional health. The Bible says we should love our neighbors as we love ourselves. So, we need to be kind to ourselves.

Be Anxious for Nothing

Don't worry about anything; instead, pray about everything. Tell God what you need, and thank him for all he has done.
Philippians 4:6 NLT

When we are expectant, we are in our waiting season; we can sometimes become anxious. When we stand in the place of prayer, trusting God to heal a patient that is so dear to us, we can get anxious. It could be a family member who is sick and dying, and we have prayed but no answer ... anxiety begins to tell on our countenance. We can carry that anxiety to our place of work, causing us to make mistakes and all sorts of human errors. When this happens, we should hold on to God's Word and continue to pray and give thanks because God has better plans, and His answer is nearer than we can imagine.

The Best Medication

But Jesus told him, "No! The Scriptures say, 'People do not live by bread alone, but by every word that comes from the mouth of God.
Matthew 4:4 NLT

The hospital is full of patients diagnosed with different illnesses and placed on different medications and prescriptions. Part of a nurse's responsibility is to ensure that patients take the right medication. While they take the pills and injections, let us try to inject the Word of God into their systems. The Bible is full of different stories of healings; let us study the Word of God, and we can give them in dozes. Give them Bible verses that pertain to their situations. For the weak, they can receive strength; the sick can receive healing, and the captive can be set free. When we feed them with the best medication (the Word of God), they will receive their healing supernaturally.

October 21

Our Declarations

No, despite all these things, overwhelming victory is ours through Christ, who loved us. Romans 8:37 NLT

Every morning we wake up, what do we stay to ourselves? When we are on clinical rotation, what do we say to the human lives God has placed right in front of us? The way we live will reflect the way we talk to others. As Christians, we should encourage others to declare whatever they want to see, not what they are going through. We become what we say. So, let us continue to declare the promises of God. Telling the patients always to say they are getting better; they are well and healed even when the test results are saying otherwise.

October 22

Nurse with A Difference

In the same way, let your good deeds shine out for all to see, so that everyone will praise your heavenly Father. Matthew 5:16 NLT

We cannot honor God with our calling, our lives, and our profession without making a difference. When God's hand is upon your life, it is glorious. When we are on duty, the whole environment will change because we carry so much joy, hope, and glory. The move of God continues to be seen in our lives on a daily basis. A nurse with a difference is one who is honoring God daily, walking with dignity and integrity, reflecting the goodness of God, and showing kindness in everything they do. To be a nurse with a difference is to love God and love others genuinely.

October 23

Drop Old Habits

This means that anyone who belongs to Christ has become a new person. The old life is gone; a new life has begun! 2 Corinthians 5:17 NLT

When we give our lives to Christ, old things pass away, and all things become new, which includes bad habits, addiction to drugs, alcohol, sexual immoralities, lying, and so on. We cannot claim to be a good Christian in public, but in the confines of our bedrooms, we are still doing the old things we did before giving our lives to Christ. We are only deceiving ourselves. We all have struggles. We need the work of the Holy Spirit daily help us to overcome the bad habits we formed in the past. Some could be lying or gossiping. Let us think about those bad habits and addictions we are struggling with and tell the Holy Spirit to help us.

Give God Your Weaknesses

He gives power to the weak and strength to the powerless.
Isaiah 40:29 NLT

The best of professionals still has their weaknesses. Nobody is perfect. Some people may claim to be perfectionists, but they still make mistakes. Regardless of our educational qualifications and skills, we still need help. God empowers us and wants us to call on Him to lean on Him where our expertise ends. Many of us make mistakes, no matter how much we try. Let us depend on God and not lean on our own understanding. Only God can transform our weaknesses into strength.

October 25

Going Above and Beyond

Work willingly at whatever you do, as though you were working for the Lord rather than for people. Remember that the Lord will give you an inheritance as your reward, and that the Master you are serving is Christ. Colossians 3:23-24 NLT

There are days when we may miss our family anniversaries, birthdays, weddings, or special moments to bond with our family members and friends. We only connect with them via social media, and our physical presence is missed by our loved ones. We often ask ourselves when we will ever get a life because 70% or more of our lives are spent in the hospital. It can be very frustrating. No one likes to miss out on social activities and family functions. In that moment of introspections, we should remember that we signed for this, and we are not missing out as sacrifice is not going in faith. On this earth, we will receive our rewards from God and favor, love, and the relationships we get from the patients are also rewarding. It is worth every sacrifice to humanity and God.

Do Not Give Up Now

Don't be afraid, for I am with you. Don't be discouraged, for I am your God. I will strengthen you and help you. I will hold you up with my victorious right hand. Isaiah 41:10 NLT

At some point in our lives, it is possible to have heard some people say they are quitting their jobs. They need to get a life, but it is not for us, as Christians. We don't stop when we are tired; we stop when we are done. God has empowered us for this assignment; we have come too far to give up. We are finishing stronger and better than we started. As the light that we are, we will shine in the darkness of sickness and disease, drawing our strength from the Holy Ghost. We are never alone. We have Christ, so we have all we need to finish this journey.

Cleanliness Is Next to Godliness

Create in me a clean heart, O God. Renew a loyal spirit within me.
Psalm 51:10 NLT

Regular cleaning in health care is essential; even more essential is personal hygiene. We cannot honor God by being dirty and untidy. We should try to be neat at all times. Wearing protective gloves, cleaning patients' vomit, urine, and blood is part of our jobs. We should be known for cleanliness. Being messy is not godly as we know that God is a God of order. We should have our uniforms neat, organized, and in order. Although for some of us, neatness may not be a natural ability, but we can learn to gradually become neat and tidy, thereby honoring God and reflecting our light as Christians.

Making God Proud

So whether we are here in this body or away from this body, our goal is to please him. 2 Corinthians 5:9 NLT

Pleasing God is our ultimate assignment as Christians. When we continue to honor God, walking in love with all men regardless of their social and financial status, we are making a bold Christian statement. We can continue to bless humanities with the way we treat others. We will treat them with patience, courtesy, and kindness, love and peace, and sensitivity. Winning souls to God on a daily basis will be our priority, and we will also make prayer our first resort and weapon. We are indeed making God proud, and His blessings will continue to chase us down. He will make our life so beautiful and decorate us with His goodness. We can make God proud by obeying His commandments and making a difference in our place of assignment.

Broken Trust

Commit everything you do to the LORD. Trust him, and he will help you. Psalms 37:5 NLT

What happens when you feel that your trust with someone has been broken? What do you do? How do you act and respond? It is hard to imagine or fathom that someone close to you would misplace your trust or take advantage of it. My troubles are not the same as your troubles and vice versa, but none the less they are troubles, and they can confuse us. Know that God is sovereign and knows what is going on in your life. He can and will handle any situation that you are currently facing. Trust that God has a reason to allow whatever it is that you are going through to occur in your life at that (this) very moment. Give praise to God for the situation and seek Him for direction. Look to God for your security in heaven, accept the pain don't resent it. There is a purpose for it in your life. GOD'S GOT IT!

October 30

Be Encouraged

As soon as I pray, you answer me; you encourage me by giving me strength. Psalm 138:3 NLT

In today's world, we need encouragement every day. As nurses, we have seen the good, the bad, and the ugly of patients and families. We've seen them born and we've seen them die. These extremes in our profession can take a toll in our everyday lives. Encourage yourself. Know that every day you go to the hospital, nursing home, or patient's home you are doing a great job. Every day won't be a walk in the park, but I encourage you to have confidence in the training that you've received.

October 31

You're More Than A Conqueror

But thank God! He has made us his captives and continues to lead us along in Christ's triumphal procession. Now he uses us to spread the knowledge of Christ everywhere, like a sweet perfume.
2 Corinthians 2:14 NLT

Every day, you are more powerful than you think. Many times, we fail to take credit for the Power that lives within us. As a believer in Christ, you have the victory in Christ Jesus. During your most difficult days, remember that you are more than a conqueror. When life seems to give you a difficult blow, remember that you are more than a conqueror. Stand tall in the power of Jesus Christ your Savior, because you are more than a conqueror.

November Health Awareness

American Diabetes

Lung Cancer Awareness

National Hospice Palliative Care

Pancreatic Cancer Awareness

Great American Smoke Out (November 19)

Walk by Faith

For we live by believing and not by seeing 2 Corinthians 5:7 NLT

When we walk by faith, we have effective faith and enduring faith. Effective faith is when you depend on God. Faith is not something we use to put on a show for others. It is complete and humble obedience to God's will and readiness to do whatever He calls us to do. The amount of faith isn't as important as the right kind of faith - faith in God. In order for our faith to grow and show evidence, it must be watered. It is watered by our daily contact with the Word and the world. The more we are in the Word, the more the world is going to come up against us. This is for our growth and development. Our faith becomes stronger through endurance. Faith means resting in what Christ has done for us in the past, but it also means hoping for what He will do for us in the future. Placing our faith in God during turbulent times builds up endurance when going through turbulent times. Continue to walk by faith and not by sight.

Are You Ready for Worship?

Sing praises to God our strength. Sing to God of Jacob.
Sing! Beat the tambourine. Play the sweet lyre and the
harp. Psalm 81:1-2 NLT

How do you prepare for Sunday morning worship? Many of us may listen to Gospel music or have private time and/or prayer time, either alone or with a prayer partner. Did you know that your preparation time in the morning will make a difference once you get to church? Moses couldn't go before the Lord without first being prepared. He had to have the right attitude and the right sacrifice (Numbers 18:1-8). Failure to have these in the right perspective would have resulted in death. What if God determined our life based on our preparation for worship? What if He decided that you didn't have the right attitude and brought the wrong sacrifice to Him? I suggest to you that before you leave your home in the morning, check your attitude and your sacrifice. Psalms 100 gives us the perfect example of what our attitude and sacrifice should be. We are to: 1. Serve the Lord with gladness; 2. Sing before His presence; 3. Enter into His gates with thanksgiving; 4. Enter into His courts with praise; 5. Bless His name. You may ask yourself, "Why should I do this?" Easy. Because God is good and His mercies are everlasting. And His truths will last for generations to come.

November 3

God Will Work It Out!

With God everything is possible. Matthew 19:16 NLT

There is a song sung by the Bonafide Praisers named "Work it Out." The song says, "Things may not be looking up but it's ok. Hold your head up high, it's gonna be a brighter day. All things work together, for good to them that love God. Whatever the situation, He will work it out."

There are many times in our lives when we feel like giving up; we feel defeated and don't know what to do. In the midst of troubling times, it is hard to see that the Apostle Paul was right in Rom. 8:28, when he says that everything works together for our good, for those that love God and who are called according to His purpose. As believers, we have to shift our focus from the problem to the Problem Solver. We must not look at the created, but we must look at the Creator, Elohim. Think about what the Apostle Paul said, in 2 Corinthians 12:9, that God's grace is sufficient and His strength is made perfect in our weakness. Know this - that no matter what the situation, God promises that He will work it out!

Broken Trust

Commit everything you do to the LORD. Trust him, and he will help you. Provers 37:5 NLT

What happens when you feel that your trust with someone has been broken? What do you do? How do you act and respond? It is hard to imagine or fathom that someone close to you would misplace your trust or take advantage of it. My troubles are not the same as your troubles, and vice versa, but nonetheless they are troubles, and they can confuse us. Know that God is sovereign and knows what is going on in your life. He can and will handle any situation that you currently face. Trust that God has a reason to allow whatever it is that you are going through to occur in your life at that (this) very moment. Give praise to God for the situation and seek Him for direction.

Allow God to mend your broken pieces. Remember what the psalm writer said in Psalm 18, The Lord is my rock, my fortress, and my savior; my God is my rock in whom I find protection. He is my shield, the power that saves me, and my place of safety. I called on the Lord, who is worthy of praise, and he saved me from my enemies.

Look to God for your security in heaven; accept the pain, don't resent it. There is a purpose for it in your life. GOD'S GOT IT!

November 5

How Long Have You Been Faithful?

The LORD's plans stand firm forever; his intentions can never be shaken. Psalm 33:11 NLT

How many years have you been faithful to God? 1 year, 2 years, 15 years, more/less? God honors faithfulness and commitment (Psalm 18:25). Don't get me wrong; we do waiver from our Christian stance from time-to- time. But we must have the desire to work at our relationship with Him. Our relationship grows when we are in a "committed" relationship with Him. Just as we sometimes date our spouses or others, we must date and court God as well. We date God daily through prayer and meditation. A "special date" would be fasting and praying. God desires to be close with us. He desires to hear the petition of our hearts. But He also desires to speak to us through His Word. How long have you been in a committed relationship with God? God's faithful promises are your shield and protection (Psalm 91:4). Cultivate your relationship with God, just as you cultivate your relationship with others.

November 6

Growing Pains

Keep your eyes on Jesus, the champion who initiates and perfects our faith. Because of the joy awaiting him, he endured the cross, disregarding its shame. Now he is seated in the place of honor beside God's throne. Hebrews 12:2 NLT

When a woman becomes pregnant, her body goes through many changes. Initially, she may experience nausea and vomiting. As the baby grows, she begins to gain weight, her body begins to expand more and more over time. Finally, she is near the time of delivery and the baby turns around in order to be birthed. These are growing pains a pregnant woman endures.

Growing pains…a necessary process in life. Remember when you were a child, and you slept for hours at a time and your parents thought that you were just being lazy? When, in fact, you were probably going through a growth spurt. During that time, you probably had some unaccounted pain. Your arms and legs hurt for no reason at all. In your Christian walk, there are growing pains, as well. There will be some physical, spiritual and emotional hurt. We have to go through these growing pains and spurts in order to bring us closer to the God we serve. Embrace the growing pains. They're for your good! Bask in the presence of the Lord to see you through this temporary valley that you're currently in. God sees you and loves you.

Intimacy with God

So, we don't look at the troubles we can see now; rather we fix our gaze on things that cannot be seen. For the things we see now will soon be gone, but the things we cannot see will last forever.
2 Corinthians 2:18 NLT

Life often gets in the way of being intimate with God. Intimacy with God requires us to acknowledge our state of being. You must admit who you are in order to move past what you are. Intimacy with God requires us to live by faith. There is no doubt that things are going to get dicey in your life. But rest assured that if you are living by faith, you can get through your tough times. Intimacy with God leads to celebration. Our time to rejoice should be all day, every day. We rejoice because these trials and tribulations are only for a short while. But you've got to remember that while you are going through those rough times and situations, you've got to give God His due in praise.

As we build our intimacy with God, we should remember what is said in 1 John 2:24-25 (NLT), So you must remain faithful to what you have been taught from the beginning. If you do, you will remain in fellowship with the Son and with the Father. And in this fellowship we enjoy the eternal life he promised us.

November 8

Forsaking All I Trust Him (F.A.I.T.H.)

This hope is a strong and trustworthy anchor for our souls.
It leads us through the curtain into God's inner sanctuary.
Hebrews 6:19 NLT

Several years ago, my husband and I had an opportunity to visit Miami for a family reunion. The water was absolutely amazing! For at least 100 yards from the beach line, you could see the bottom of the ocean. While we were wading in the water, looking over the sea, the sky began to change. Previously you could see the shoreline of all the buildings. But then they were gone in the middle of the clouds. While I was watching the sky, I felt the water changing. The waves began to pick up and became choppy and rough. As I felt the change in the water and the change in the sky, an old-time song came to me: "There's a storm out over the ocean and it's movin' this-a-way, if your soul's not anchored in Jesus, you will surely drift away." It really got me to thinking about life's ups and downs, trials and tribulations and stormy seas. If you are not secured in and have a relationship with Christ, if you are not anchored in Jesus, then the stormy sea of your life will sweep you away into the ocean, or it will take you with the current and you could drown. I encourage you to STAND UP in Jesus. Know and understand that He is your source and resource for all that you go through. Keep the F.A.I.T.H. (forsaking all I trust Him).

November 9

Let God Do His Job

Dear friends, never take revenge. Leave that to the righteous anger of God. For the Scriptures say, I will take revenge; I will pay them back, says the LORD. Romans 12:19 NLT

Has there ever been a time in your life where you tried to get revenge? C'mon, be honest. C'mon…. OK! If you didn't try to get revenge, you thought about getting revenge. You thought about how you could bring some kind of disaster to the person who hurt you. Our purpose as believers is not to seek revenge. Throughout the Scriptures, revenge is not ours but the Lord's. As believers, our responsibility is to trust and believe that God has our back. God truly understands and knows our plight. Does getting revenge on someone who has hurt us really beneficial? Seriously? I must admit - getting immediate satisfaction sounds good. But knowing that God has my back and will settle any dispute and/or problem for me sounds really great. Over the years, I, like you, have had people do wrong against me. But I've never taken revenge. I've thought about it. But I've never done it. What I have done was watch the hand of God take care of the situation and/or the people involved in the situation. God looks out for those whom He calls His children. So, we don't have to seek revenge on those who may have done wrong against us. Our responsibility is to be obedient, to study His Word, pray and meditate. So, don't seek revenge. Allow God to handle your case. He's the judge and the jury. Let Him do His job, and you do yours.

November 10

Watch Your Mouth

Don't use foul or abusive language. Let everything you say be good and helpful, so that your words will be an encouragement to those who hear them. Ephesians 4:29 NLT

Kind words heal and help; cutting word wound and maim Proverbs 15:4 (MSG).

As Christians, many of us grumble and complain about a number of things regarding the church, church work and church folk. We say things like, "They get on my nerves. She always has to be in the middle of something. He/she thinks they are in charge 'cuz pastor isn't here." We're all guilty of this (or something like this) in the past. However, this is not building up the Kingdom of God. In fact, this tears the Kingdom apart. Our responsibility is to speak kindly to one another and build each other up, not down. So, as you come and go, and you hear another believer begin to tear down a fellow saint, kindly and gently remind him/her of what Ephesians 4:29 says. In fact, when he/she begins to speak negatively, simply say 429, and take him/her to the passage.

BE ENCOURAGED.

Remember this, encourage each other and build each other up, just as you are already doing (1 Thessalonians 5:11). Don't be discouraged. Continue to be the best representation of Christ that you can be.

November 11

Change Isn't Easy

For everything there is a season, a time for every activity under heaven. Ecclesiastes 3:1 NLT

Change isn't easy for anyone. Many times, it's something that we don't want or plan to happen. We get complacent and comfortable in our position. So, my question for you is, what do you need to do in order to change? I propose that only God can make a change in your life. Change happens when you allow God's truth to be written upon your heart (Prov. 3:3-4). Once the truth is written upon your heart, you can begin to change and transform (Rom. 12:1-2). While we are allowing God to write the truth upon our hearts, and the truth is transforming us; that very truth now breeds freedom (2 Cor. 3:17b-18). Oh, to be free: from agony, from hurt, from pain, from depression, from disappointments, from everything. No one said that change would be easy. Just remember that where the Spirit of the Lord is, there is liberty (freedom). We may not understand why we are going through the things that we are going through, but God does, and He is working it all out for us.

November 12

Jubilee

It will be a jubilee year for you, and you must keep it holy.
Leviticus 25:12a NLT

What does a celebratory year look like to you? Did you get married? Have a child? Get a new job? Celebrate a milestone in marriage or birthday? Whatever it was that occurred, smiles, laughter and joy were in the air, you were with family, friends, co-workers and fellow believers. Whomever you were with made that moment even more exciting. I know you're smiling right now. Keep doing it. A smile on the outside can make you heart smile on the inside.

Jubilee means a joyful shout or banging of trumpets. In biblical times, it occurred in the 50th year. As one moves forward in life, one thinks about the milestones that have occurred. There were some good days and some not so good. I want to encourage you that your Jubilee is coming. Wait for it. When it arrives, make sure you make a joyful noise unto the Lord, for He is worthy to be praised.

November 13

Obedience

Even though Jesus was God's Son, he learned obedience from the things he suffered. Hebrews 5:8 NLT

Tough decisions can make you feel like giving up. Tough decisions can make you feel like throwing in the towel. But each of us has a calling in our lives to be obedient to the will of God.

There are times in life when we just want to be rebellious. We don't want to follow the rules. We drive over the speed limit. We take short cuts in order to get through something faster. However, being obedient is what God desires for our lives. He wants us to be obedient to His will and His way. Our obedience to God doesn't always feel good; in fact, sometimes it's even painful. But I'm reminded that even in those painful moments, God has me on His mind, and all things will be alright according to His plan and His purpose.

November 14

Newness

For I am about to do something new. See, I have already begun!
Do you not see it? Isaiah 43:19a NLT

I remember my one and only brand new car. It was a blue Geo Storm 5-speed with a blue interior. Nice and shiny. It had that classic new car smell, like they just took it off the assembly line. I felt like a new woman with a new car. That's how I felt when I rededicated my life to Christ. I felt brand new in His sight. It doesn't mean that it has to be anything grand or glorious or showy. It may very well be something small and delicate. Nevertheless, it is something new. What are some of the things that are new? Let's keep it simple: God gave us brand new grace and mercy when you woke up! Isn't that GRAND? I hope you're excited about the new things that come your way each and every day.

When you dedicate your life to Christ, something on the inside changes the trajectory of your life. God is doing something new, in YOU!

November 15

Affection

Love each other with genuine affection, and take delight in honoring each other. Romans 12:10 NLT

What does it mean to be in love? To be affectionate to someone else? Affection doesn't necessarily mean romance. Affection can be between friends or siblings. Every one desires affection of some sort. We want it from our spouses, children, friends and loved ones. But, for some of us, it's hard to give affection to others. Those we've sought affection from are also, at times, the those who may have hurt us. I suggest to you that you seek the face of Jesus. In your loneliest moments, seek Jesus. When you feel abandoned, seek Jesus. God is the Father to the fatherless and Mother to the motherless. He promised to be with you at all times. He ultimately desires your affection at all times. Love God with all of your heart and all of your soul. Take the time to be in the presence of God through prayer, study and meditation.

God's presence has never left you, even when you thought it was your darkest night or the deepest whole. Hold tight to God's hand. Don't doubt His presence nor His power. God will not let you down.

November 16

Nurturing

Give all your worries and cares to God, for he cares about you.
1 Peter 5:7 NLT

What does nurturing mean to you? What does it look like in your day-to-day life? When we think of someone or something that is nurturing, we often look at mothers and their children. They care for and nurture the children that surround them. But do you know that even those who don't have children of their own are nurturers as well? Nurturing comes from the desire to care for others, not simply because they were blessed to have a child. God is the ultimate nurturer. He desires to care for His children in the good days as well as the bad. He cares for you when you're up and when you're down. He wants to comfort you in every aspect of your life. Look toward God to nurture your soul. Cast your cares towards God, for He cares for you.

I wonder why you care, God—why do you bother with us at all? All we are is a puff of air; we're like shadows in a campfire. Research all the way from sky to sea; pull me out of the ocean of hate, out of the grip of the ocean of hate, out of the grip of those barbarians (Psalm 144:3-4, 7).

November 17

New Life

You were dead because of your sins and because your sinful nature was not yet cut away. Then God made you alive with Christ, for he forgave all our sins. He canceled the record of the charges against us and took it away by nailing it to the cross.
Colossians 2:13-14 NLT

When was the last time you held a new born baby? They smell so good! When you look in their face, you can't help but to smile. It makes me think about all of the potential they have going forward in life. The new friends they will make. The school projects and activities they'll participate in. It gives me warm fuzzies all over.

When we accept Christ as Lord and Savior into our lives, we became new creatures (2 Corinthians 5:17) our old nature (pre-salvation) has gone away. Prior to our conversion, we were dead, because our sin nature had not been taken away. But after salvation, our life became new. We had new beginnings in and through Christ Jesus. All of this was done because of Christ dying on the cross for our sins. Bask in the newness that is in Christ Jesus. New life in Him is something to celebrate.

November 18

Attraction

You should clothe yourselves instead with the beauty that comes from within, the unfading beauty of a gentle and quiet spirit, which is so precious to God. 1 Peter 3:4 NLT

The evil queen from the animated movie Snow White once said, "Mirror, mirror on the wall, who's the fairest of them all?"

Go to the nearest mirror. Go ahead; go look. What do you see? Some of you have light skin or dark skin. Some have straight hair or curly hair or somewhere in between. Take another look in the mirror; but this time, try to look deep in your soul. Do you see the light shining bright? That's the Son shining through you. The Son (Jesus) that shines inside of you shines brighter than the sun in the sky. When the Holy Spirit came into your life, He created an attraction that is indescribable. Has anyone ever said to you, "There's something different about you? I can't put my fingers on it." My sister and my brother, that "something different" is the Light of the Holy Spirit shining bright! Don't worry about what's on the outside when you look in the mirror - love the person that's on the inside, that shines bright with the love of Jesus!

November 19

Beautiful

Yet God has made everything beautiful for its own time.
Ecclesiastes 3:11a NLT

There's an old saying: "Beauty is in the eyes of the beholder." Did you know that when you were created, God made you beautiful, just the way you are? You may say to yourself, "I have scars. I'm fat. I'm too tall. I'm too short." My beloved, no matter how you look on the outside, God looks at the inside. And because God doesn't make any mistakes, He made you beautiful just the way you are.

Your beauty has the possibility to be a positive effect on those that surround you. Your inner strength when you face the craziness of life has the ability to help and lift someone else who's going through a crazy time as well. 1 Peter 3:3-4 gives us great instruction. He tells us not to focus on outer beauty. We, as believers, should be known for our inner beauty that is unfading, gentle and quiet. These are attributes that are pleasing to God.

Rewards

But as for you, be strong and courageous, for your work will be rewarded. 2 Chronicles 15:7 NLT

Faith is to believe what you do not see; the reward of this faith is to see what you believe. ~Saint Augustine

Have you participated in group sports or activities, such as chess, debate team, marching band, etc.? At the conclusion of the game or tournament, a winner is announced. Usually, there is first, second or third place awards. All who landed in those categories receive some time of trophy, ribbon or plaque. The first-place winner typically gets the biggest prize. As a team, that's what we strive for with the event. In Christ, our reward isn't earthly, but heavenly. In other words, the earthly rewards are temporary, whereas the heavenly rewards last forever and ever. Temporary rewards fade away, just as the grass withers away after time. But an eternal reward can never dull, dwindle or disappear. Your eternal reward is given by God. Be encouraged - your Christian walk has not gone unnoticed by God. He will give you the ultimate reward when you see Him face-to-face.

November 21

Yearn

As the deer longs for streams of water, so I long for you, O God. I thirst for God, the living God. When can I go and stand before him? Psalm 42:1-2 NLT

The fact is, everything we want or yearn for is won through other people. No man on an island is happy; he is merely existing. The joyous life is the one filled with rich relationships. ~ Vernon Howard

Have you ever been thirsty? I mean, really thirsty. The more you drank, the more you needed to drink. When the body has a great need to drink continuously, the body is, in fact, dehydrated. The automatic response is to feed it liquid (soda, Gatorade, alcohol, etc.). But what the body really needs is water. Good, old fashioned H_2O. So, it is with our relationship with God. Our soul pants like a deer who needs water to survive. Our inner man connected to Christ yearns to be in the presence of the Lord. There are times when our yearning for the Lord is greater than others. But just like the deer desires the streams of water, so does the heart of the believer seek Him diligently, both day and night. Take a moment to sit still and meditate on the goodness of God. Ask Him for the peace that you desire in your life.

November 22

Accessible

But if you remain in me and my words remain in you, you may ask for anything you want, and it will be granted. John 15:7 NLT

What does it mean to be accessible? According to the Merriam-Webster Dictionary Online, in reference to a person, it is typically a person who is in a position of authority or importance. When I was a director of nursing for a nursing home, I had an open-door policy, which simply meant that if someone needed to meet with me, he/she had access. That was for work. But what about after work? How accessible are you? Sometimes, we are too accessible to people. We're accessible to our spouses, children and work. But how accessible are you to God? When we make ourselves too accessible to others, we decrease the amount of time we have for God. We're working overtime, kids are in three extracurricular activities each - six out of seven days a week - and our spouses demand one date night a week. I implore you to make yourself accessible to God. He desires to abide, commune and communicate to and with you every day. Seek God's face. There's no better place to be than in the presence of God the Father.

November 23

Noiseless

In peace I will lie down and sleep, for you alone, O LORD, will keep me safe. Psalm 4:8 NLT

Little children are noisy. It's their nature. The giggle, squeal, and scream. Sometimes for no reason. Many adults then say in turn, "Ugghh, it's too noisy in here! Stop all that noise!"

As adults, there will always be people talking all around you. Your neighbors are having a party in the middle of the week, like it's a summer holiday. People in your workspace are all on the phone at the same time, and Lord, the humans in your house just won't keep quiet to save their lives.

Many times, in your life, the noise that surrounds you is overwhelming. In many cases, excessive noise drowns out what God is saying to us in the present season of life. Near the end of Jesus' earthly ministry, He often we go to a quiet place to pray to His Father (Luke 5:16). I encourage you to find a still space, car, room, bathroom, basement, etc. and have a talk with Jesus. Tell Him the things you can't tell anyone else. Enjoy the silent, noiseless moments of your life. Embrace it as God comforts you.

November 24

Thankful

Don't fret or worry. Instead of worrying, pray. Let petitions and praises shape your worries into prayers, letting God know your concerns. Before you know it, a sense of God's wholeness, everything coming together for good will come and settle you down. It's wonderful what happens when Christ displaces worry at the center of your life. Philippians 4:6-7 MSG

November has been designated our month of reflecting and giving thanks. We often gather with friends and family for a great Thanksgiving Day feast. But, as the years go by, we move further and further away from reflecting on the things in our lives we are to be thankful for. What are we to be thankful for? Everything and everyone (1 Thessalonians 5:18). Give thanks to God, our creator. Give thanks to God, our healer. Give thanks to God, our provider. A thankful heart is a grateful heart. Give thanks for the small things and the big things. I am thankful to you for making it this far. Keep pushing. You can do it!

Remember this: Give thanks to the LORD and proclaim his greatness. Let the whole world know what he has done(Psalm 105:1 NLT).

November 25

Joy

I will be filled with joy because of you. I will sing praises to your name, O Most High. Psalm 9:2 NLT

When a person gets excited about something, he/she's whole demeanor changes. He/she smiles more. The wrinkles in his/her forehead seem to disappear. He/she seems more relaxed. He/she is actually pleasant to be around. One could say he/she was happy and another could say he/she was joyful. Happiness generally occurs when something positive happens, such as you close on a house or got a new car. Joy occurs regardless of what happens. Joy is not something that you inherit. It's not something that occurs simply because of the smile you have on your face. For the believer, joy is internal. Joy is because of our savior. Joy occurs whether we're up or down. Joy is because our faith lies in the fact that we have hope in Christ. In other words, joy is Jesus.

The Christian songwriter Darrell Evan wrote, *Trading My Sorrows.* It Has been sung and recorded by many artists, include Israel Houghton. The first verse says, I'm trading my sorrows; I'm trading my shame; I'm laying them down for the joy of the Lord. What an exciting song to sing. When it seems like the world is crashing around you, think about this song. Trade in all of those things that bog you down for the joy of the Lord.

Laughter is Great Medicine

We were filled with laughter, and we sang for joy. And the other nations said, "What amazing things the LORD has done for them." Psalm 126:2 NLT

Years ago, Tickle Me Elmo® for children was hot on the market. You saw the commercials on television of children holding Elmo and laughing. I didn't understand it until I went to the toy store to go Christmas shopping for my nieces and nephews. I saw Elmo in the store, picked him up and he started laughing. Subsequently, so did I. Nothing was funny except the fact that Elmo was laughing. It was amazing how great I felt when it was over. During the darkest of dark days, when you feel like you can't take another step, I encourage you to look at a comedy show, play with a child. Reflect on something that occurred in the past that made you laugh. Maybe it was something silly from childhood. But whatever it is, laugh as hard and as frequently as you can. Point to yourself and say, if I've made it this far, I can keep going!

King David reminds us of this in Psalm 30:4-5 (MSG), All you saints! Sing your hearts out to God! Thank him to his face! He gets angry once in a while, but across a lifetime there is only love. The nights of crying your eyes out give way to days of laughter.

November 27

You are Different

You are a royal priests, a holy nation, God's very own possession. As a result, you can show others the goodness of God, for he called you out of the darkness into his wonderful light. 1 Peter 2:9 NLT

Do you know that you are different, special even? Yes, I'm talking to you. God knew about you before the beginning of the world. He knew about the highs and the lows that you were going to have to endure. But when He created you, He broke the mold. There is no one else like you. You, my friend, as a believer in Christ, are a King's kid. Ma'am, you are a princess. Sir, you are a prince. You are of royal priesthood. You are special in God's sight. He created you in His own image. Does that mean you're perfect? No, it simply means God had you in mind when He created you. In other words, God knew you before the foundation of the world (Ephesians 1:4). He created us to be different and set apart from others. Hold your head high and stand tall. Know that with God, all things are possible! Don't conform to this world. Transform your mind by studying God's word and living according to His precepts. Continue to be set aside for the work of the ministry. Continue to be different. You are part of God's family.

Pleasing God

When people's lives please the LORD, even their enemies are at peace with them. Proverbs 16:7 NLT

Many of us grew up wanting to please our parents. When we did things in our lives, we wanted to be sure that they were proud of us. We wanted them to be pleased with our grades. We wanted them to be pleased when we cleaned our rooms or helped out at dinner time. Ultimately, we didn't want to get into trouble with our parents. Pleasing God is really no different. We want God to be pleased with the things that we do and say throughout our lives. When we feel that we have not pleased Him, we are shameful and want to hide. But to please God is to obey God. True obedience is pleasing God. Joshua 1:8 says: Study the Book of the Law continually. Meditate on it, day and night, so you may be sure to obey all that is written in it. Only then will you succeed. You see, without obedience to God, there is no success. There may be earthly success, but you can't take that with you to heaven. In fact, earthly obedience really doesn't mean a lot to God. He wants all of us, our whole being, to be obedient. We can't continue to give Him lip service and think that He is pleased with us, can we? James 1:22 says, in part, that we are to be doers of the Word of God and not just hearers. God wants more from us than what we currently give. Are you willing to change in order to please God?

November 29

Don't Be Afraid

They do not fear bad news; they confidently trust the LORD to care for them. Psalm 112:7 NLT

Too many times, we are afraid to do something for fear of what the outcome may be. We're afraid to change jobs because we don't know if we will be successful. We don't get out of a bad relationship because we are afraid of being alone. In 1 Samuel 17, you'll find the story of David and Goliath. It is amazing how a young boy would go up to a giant when grown men were afraid to do so. When he went to face Goliath, David was fitted with only five smooth stones, a sling and a shepherd's staff, while Goliath had a "guard" with a shield in front of him and was fitted with a breastplate, helmet and sword. Just like Goliath, Satan taunts us daily about that one thing we are afraid of facing. Sometimes, he really gets on our nerves, and we fall for the "okie doke" and get caught up in his nonsense. But just like David was armed with the proper gear, so are we: THE BIBLE, GOD'S HOLY WORD. 2 Timothy 1:7 says that God did not give the spirit of fear; He gave us power, love and a sound mind. He has empowered us to do great things, in His name and power. Don't be afraid to step out on faith and do what God has destined you to do.

When Trouble Comes

O God, listen to my cry! Hear my prayer! From the ends of the earth, I cry to you for help when my heart is overwhelmed. Lead me to the towering rock of safety, for you are my safe refuge, a fortress where my enemies cannot reach me. Psalm 61:1-3 NLT

An old Negro spiritual says, in part, "Nobody knows the trouble I've seen. Nobody knows my sorrow." Many times in life, we feel no one understands what's happening with us. No one understands the trouble that plagues your mind and soul. I'm here to tell you that Jesus knows all about it.

Trouble seems to find us, particularly when we're not looking. There are days when we seemingly are minding our own business and life happens: someone close to us passes away, we get behind on a major bill, we become ill and can't work, etc.... Whatever it is, it seems to knock us down. I encourage you to get up and fight! Tell yourself that trouble doesn't always last. Tell yourself that God is very present to help in times of trouble. He will guide you along the way. Our responsibility is to cry out to God. I promise - He does hear you, even when you think He doesn't. Cry. Scream. Yell. Do whatever you think you need to do. But at the end of the day, pray. Pray for God to give you comfort and to see you through your darkest days.

December Health Awareness

World AIDS Day (December 1)

National Handwashing Awareness Week (December 6-12)

December 1

Issues

Even when I walk through the darkest valley, I will not be afraid, for you are close beside me. Your rod and your staff protect and comfort me. Psalm 23:4 NLT

Many times, as believers, we wonder how others get through their issues. Not small issues, but big issues that can derail one's faith. The answer is they have a sound foundation in the Bible. In Deuteronomy 6, God told the children of Israel through Moses that they were to teach the generations about what took place in the past. But more importantly, they were to teach them about God's law. They were going to a land where there were good things. There would be wells they didn't have to dig and land that was already available for them. But when they got there, they weren't supposed to forget God. That's what we need to remember. When we are in our valley moments, they are just that - a moment. We have to dig deep on the Word that's within us. I encourage you to read and study your Bible as often as you can. You never know when you will be in a valley moment and need the will of the living God to help.

Be encouraged; God is still on the throne

December 2

Even me

For God loved the world so much that he gave his one and only Son, so that everyone who believes in him will not perish but have eternal life. John 3:16 NLT

Crystal Aikin, one of Sunday's Best winners, sings a song, "Even Me." In this song, she speaks about how God continues to want to use you even though there are times in which you were identified with faults, brokenness, unworthiness and guilty stains. Most times, we fall and refuse to get up. Many times, we are weak and discouraged by our situation. But our God, despite our imperfections, still chooses to use you. Because God chose to use you and me is a reason for us to be excited. Remember, it is because of the blood of Jesus that our sins are washed away. The penalty associated with being a sinner is no longer there. Thank God for the blood of Jesus. When Satan accuses you of horrible crimes, know that Jesus stands before God and says, "I've got them covered." And because of this, He still can use you, regardless of your imperfections. Continue to stand and be used by God. Face your fears. Remember Christ died on the cross for you to live.

December 3

You Are A Survivor

I'm asking God for one thing, only one thing: To live with him in his house my whole life long. I'll contemplate his beauty; I'll study at his feet. Psalm 27:4 MSG

Throughout this journal, you'll find various subjects recognizing health/disease awareness, such as heart disease, sickle cell, lupus, arthritis, etc. A number of people suffer from any one of them or know someone that does. My point is that they or you have survived, are surviving or will survive "your" disease. We're not defined by the disease or consequence of our lives. Too often, we allow others to define us by our disease or circumstance. You, my friend, are a survivor. Whatever it is that you are facing, you can survive it. No matter how big or small it is, God is with you. When folks turn their backs on you, stand tall, because you are a survivor. When your loved ones seem to do you wrong, stand tall, because you are a survivor. When the turmoils of life seem to knock you around, get back up, look whatever IT is in the face, and say, If God is for us, who can ever be against us (Romans 8:31b NLT)? I AM A SURVIVOR!

December 4

You're Free

Now the Lord is that Spirit: and where the Spirit of the Lord is, there is liberty. 2 Corinthians 3:17 NLT

Singing: I'm free, Praise the Lord, I'm free. No longer bound. No more chains hold me. It's a blessing, such a blessing. Praise the Lord, hallelujah, I'm free.

Too many times, as believers, we forget that we are free in Christ. John 8:36 says, in part, if Jesus made you free, then you are free indeed. This doesn't mean that we can do what we want to do and how we want to do it without consequences. Unlike other religions, being Christ-like incorporates free will. Although you may do whatever you choose to do, there is and will be consequences regarding that decision. But rest assured, when you confess your sins and turn away from that which displeases God and turn to Him in repentance, your sins shall be forgiven. Remember what Apostle Paul tells us in Galatians 5:1 (MSG), Christ has set us free to live a free live. So, take your stand! Never again let anyone put a harness of slavery on you.

Stand up and declare, I'M FREE!

December 5

You Are Strong

*So be strong and courageous, all you who put your hope in the
LORD! Psalm 31:24 NLT*

At one time, Arnold Schwarzenegger could deadlift 710 pounds. Jackie O
exhibited great strength after the assignation of her husband, President John
F. Kennedy. The mother who has buried her child displayed strength when
she got out of the bed the next day. A husband who buried his wife after 60
years of marriage showed strength when he picked out her clothes for the
funeral. You are stronger than you look. I know it doesn't always feel like
it. In fact, sometimes, our weakness seems like it overpowers us. But you,
my friend, have a secret weapon; your secret weapon is prayer, study on
God's Word and to meditate and commune with God. That's where inner
strength comes from. If we rely on ourselves, it would never get done. But
when you rely on the strength that lies within, nothing can stop you! Always
remember Proverbs 3:5-6: "Trust in the Lord with all your heart and lean
not on your own understanding; in all your ways acknowledge him, and he
shall direct thy paths."

December 6

No Judgement Zone

And Saul said to David "You are not able to go against this Philistine to fight with him; for you are a youth, and he a man of war from his youth." 1 Samuel 17:33

Do you remember the story of David and Goliath (1 Samuel 17)? David was chosen by God to be king. But there was a hiccup in the process. The people chose Saul in the interim. While King Saul was running the country, David tended to the sheep of his father, Jesse. There came a time when the Philistine people raised issues with Israel and brought forth Goliath to handle the matter. The people were scared and thought they would perish at Goliath's hand. But David came forth to say, "I'll take care of the problem." King Saul said to David, in part, you're too small; you're too young; he's too strong and mighty. But David had faith that Yahweh was on his side. He didn't allow other's opinion and judgement of him deter him from doing what was necessary to save his people. Too often, we allow the naysayers and doubters in our ear to turn us away from what God had instructed us to do and where to go. I implore you to move when God says move. Don't allow anyone to discourage or distract you. Don't allow him/her to tell you that you're too old or you're too young to do what God says. Your life is in God's hand; you can do all things through Christ.

Praise Challenge

Then David danced before the LORD with all his might.
2 Samuel 6:14a NKJV

Dr. Veirdre Jackson once said, "Peace isn't passive. It's active and bold. It's a shift, a stance and a weapon." How is it active? It's an exchange between the Holy Spirit and you. You actively seek it and He actively gives it. It's a bold declaration in your life. It stands up out front, even when you feel defeated. It's a shift in authority, because God is ultimately in control and not you. You're giving Him control over the space and situation. It's a stance in the face of fear. When that "thing" creeps up in your life that makes you tremble, it's the peace of God that allows you to face whatever is going on. Finally, it's a weapon, from God above. It's a weapon, because God holds the fate of your life. It is ultimately all in His hands.

So, when you are feeling panicked because of what life throws your way, don't fret - seek God's face and peace. When you feel the world is against you, don't fret - seek the peace that surpasses all understanding. When you feel that the world is crumbling all around you, ask God to wrap His peace all around you as you face the challenging moment. And when it's all said and done, give God the best praise dance you have deep in your soul. I promise that when it's all over, there will be a comforting deep down within that will be indescribable except to say, BUT GOD!!

December 8

Submission

And if you do not carry your own cross and follow me, you cannot be my disciple. Luke 14:27 NLT

Submit and surrender. It is something that all persons have a difficult time with no matter who you are, man or woman, married or single. None of us wants to surrender or submit to anything or anyone. Many of us view it as a sign of weakness. We may view it as giving up who we are as a person. That is not the case at all. Submission in the Christian worldview is different than the worldly view. The world often views submission as someone being in charge over your very being; telling you what to do every step of the way. But that is not how God intended for it to be. Submission is mutual; the husband submits to the wife and vice versa. Submission works to smooth functioning in areas like business, government or the family. Submission and surrender are not bad things; they are actually a good thing in the sight of God.

Remember this, Start with God—the first step in learning is bowing down to God; only fools thumb their noses at such wisdom and learning (Proverbs 1:7 MSG).

Pray Until Something Happens (P.U.S.H.)

I press on to reach the end of the race and receive the heavenly
prize for which God, through Christ Jesus is calling us.
Philippians 3:14 NLT

Many, many moons ago, I ran track in high school. I can't say that I was the fastest person out there, but I strived to be. At the end of the race, the official would ask for your name if you came in first, second or third place. In any of these three positions, your name was placed in the local newspaper for the whole town to see. That was the prize: "notoriety." That's an earthly prize. But as believers, we are to seek the heavenly "prize."

P.U.S.H. gives the implication that you actually have to do something. You can't just sit there like a bump on a log. Get up, and P.U.S.H. God didn't direct us to sit on our do-nothings just to wait for something to happen. We have a responsibility. We are to pray fervently and frequently. In fact, we should pray without ceasing. God knows the desires of our heart. He also knows what's best for us. Your responsibility is to P.U.S.H. Seek God's face until it's clear what God wants you to say and/or do. Pray and watch God change things!

December 10

Intentional Faith

Therefore, put on every piece of God's armor so you will be able to resist the enemy in the time of evil. Then after the battle you will still be standing firm. Ephesians 5:13 NLT

Imagine, if you will, the solider preparing to go into an impeding battle or war. He/she must be prepared with all necessary tactical gear. He/she must have the proper footwear, headgear and body gear. He/she must also have faith that at the end of the day, he/she will return to his/her bunker, safe and sound. Faith is not passive. Faith is active. Faith is purposeful. Faith is intentional.

Paul tells us that after we get our life in God's order, we need to have intentional strength. We are to be strong, not in our own strength, but in the strength of the Lord. We must remember our Christian strength lies in our daily communication with the Lord. Intentional power in the might of God is nothing that we can do on our own. It's all in the hands of our mighty God. When you have intentional strength in the Lord and intentional power by His might, you will then have resilient faith in Christ. No matter what happens in life, remember that with God by your side, you can bounce back from anything, because you have intentional, resilient faith.

December 11

Positive Attitude

Think about things that are excellent and worthy of praise.
Philippians 4:8c NLT

Have you ever said to someone, "You have an attitude problem?" This usually means that the person has some sort of chip on his/her shoulder or something is bothering him/her that gives the impression of a negative attitude. There will always be days when things don't seem to work out the way we want them to. But, as believers, we must do our best to have a positive attitude. What can a positive attitude do for you? It allows God to work, even in the most disappointing times. Think about Joseph and his brothers (Genesis 39). Joseph was placed in an ugly position, but there's no evidence that he displayed a negative attitude. He trusted that Yahweh would work things out in his favor. A positive attitude can have an impact on others. Think about it like this - a positive attitude is like an infectious laugh. It spreads from person-to-person, even if he/she doesn't want it to. A positive attitude helps when facing difficult times. Every one of us has had challenges in life. Some of them were big, others were small. But nevertheless, they were difficult times. A positive attitude can make the difficult times manageable. Think about the three Hebrew boys (Daniel 3). They were in a bad situation. But their attitude was not that of a dismal mindset. Instead, they turned their situation over to God to work it all out. As believers, we must internalize and exude a positive attitude towards any given situation. We may not know what the outcome will be in the end. But we can truly say to ourselves, "Thy will be done, Lord, in all things."

December 12

Got Faith

Now faith is the substance of things hoped for, the evidence of things not seen. Hebrews 11:1 NLT

According to Hebrews 11, we can't see faith. It's invisible, intangible. We can't put our fingers on it. But when you have effective and active faith, it depends on and in God to do the impossible. A small amount of genuine faith in God takes root and grows. Initial faith, almost invisible at first, begins to spread and then becomes noticeable to others. Soon, this faith will have produced major results that will uproot and destroy competing loyalties. We don't need more faith; a tiny seed of faith is enough if it is alive and growing. We need to exercise our faith. We need to put it into action.

How do we put faith into action? It's like riding a bike. Initially you may need to use training wheels and you're unsettled. But, eventually, you start to get the hang of it, and then the training wheels come off and you're on your own. You're nervous, wobbly and you may even fall down. But you dust yourself off and get back up and start over. Our faith initially may be off-centered. But continued prayer, study of God's word and meditation will help you to strengthen your faith day-by-day and moment-by-moment.

December 13

Faith on Repeat

He prayed three times a day, just as he had always done, giving thanks to his God. Daniel 6:10b NLT

Imagine, if you will, a hamster in a cage on the hamster wheel. He keeps going around and around. Day in and day out, the hamster gets on the wheel. It doesn't matter if it's raining outside or if it's 100 degrees, he faithfully gets on that wheel. That's how we should be with our faith.

Day in and day out, situations arise. Trials and tribulations will come your way. That's a fact. It's just a way of life. But, as believers, we have to put our faith on repeat, just like Daniel did in the Bible. Our need to search for God needs to be on repeat. We need to seek God's face daily. We need to pray about everything. Don't leave anything unturned. Turn it over to the Lord and leave it there. Be obedient. Don't bow to the crazy circumstances and situations in your life. Be obedient to God's Word. Remember - God's got your back. And if you stumble and fall, do it all over again.

Put your faith on repeat.

December 14

I Still Have Joy

Come, let us tell of the LORD's greatness; let us exalt his name together. Psalm 34:3 NLT

If you've ever failed a test in school, raise your hand. If you've ever had an argument or disagreement with your spouse, raise your hand. If you've ever been heart broken, raise your hand. Those examples - and others - were times in your life that were challenging and disappointing. On some occasions, you felt down and discouraged and didn't feel as though you had any joy left in your life. But there is hope on the horizon. You still can have joy, despite what it looks like.

So, how can we still have joy, despite what it looks like? Simple. First, you must bless the Lord. Do this in good times and in bad times. Remember, God is worthy to be praised. Second, despite what it looks like, boast about the goodness of God. Even though the world seems like it's falling apart, boasting or bragging about what God has done will boost your spirits and change your focus. Finally, magnify the Lord. Remember, God is bigger than your problems and your situations. Turn it over to the Lord and leave it there. He is your way maker, your shelter and your peace. Despite what it looks like, you still have joy.

This Is Only A Test

If we are thrown into the blazing furnace, the God whom we serve
is able to save us. He will rescue us from your power, Your
Majesty. Daniel 3:17 NLT

Periodically, throughout the day, since 1963, the emergency broadcast system sends a signal through the airways on television and the radio. They send an eerie sound to get the viewer's and/or listener's attention. At the conclusion of the 30-60 second test, they would indicate the test was over and what would have happened if it were a true emergency. The announcer simply said, "This is only a test."

Life is not easy. Things seem to go wrong all at the same time. Remember, this (life) is only a test. When you find that things are not going the way that you wanted them to go, does your effective faith grow under pressure (Daniel 3:1-16)? As things pile up on us, we must remember that God is still standing with us. When, day after day and night after night, there seems to be no relief, know that effective faith becomes stronger through endurance (Daniel 3:17). Without a test, there is no testimony. Rest assured, when the devil decides to throw his fiery arrows your way, your effective faith is a quiet certainty, and that with God on your side, you can't fail. Keep the faith. Keep the focus. Remember, this is only a test.

December 16

Jovial

Happy are those who hear the joyful call to worship, for they will walk in the light of your presence, LORD. Psalm 89:15 NLT

George W. Cooke wrote a children's song titled, "I've Got the Joy." It simply says, in part, I've got the joy down in my heart to stay. There, of course, are more words to this song, but you get the picture. The joy that Mr. Cooke was referring to is the joy of the Lord. This Jesus-joy is irreplaceable. No matter what happens, the joy of the Lord is upon those that believe.

Another word for joy is jovial, which means cheerful or happy. What types of feelings do you have when you think about being in worship with the Lord? The thought of being in worship with the Lord brings a smile to my face. The idea of communing with God, just Him and me, brings me comfort and peace. Take a few moments to reflect on Psalm 85:15. If you're happy in Jesus, you'll walk in the light and in the presence of the Lord.

December 17

Omnipotent

I will steady him with my hand; with my powerful arm I will make him strong. Psalm 89:21 NLT

Many children enjoy going to or watching the circus. They're amazed by the animals, clowns, music, etc. One act that amazed them was the man who could lift 700-pounds. The children's eyes would light up in disbelief. Some would yell, "You're really strong! How did you get that way?" While others would say, "I want to be strong and powerful like you when I grow up one day!" The Person who is more strong and powerful than the most powerful man on earth is God the father. God is omnipotent (all-powerful). The strength of His hand is able to destroy anything and cure everything. When reflecting on God's omnipotent power, I feel safe and secure. At those moments in your life when you feel the world is overpowering you, think about the powerful hand of God comforting you and holding you safely in His arms. Lay your head on God's shoulder and remember that it's all in His hands. He controls it all. God is all powerful at all times.

December 18

Noble

Who may worship in your sanctuary, Lord? Who may enter your presence on your holy hill? Those who lead blameless lives and do what is right, speaking the truth from sincere hearts.
Psalm 15:1-2 NLT

King David asks two questions here: who may worship in His sanctuary and who can be in His presence. He tells us plainly the types of people who are able to do this. Those who lead blameless lives, do right, speak truth with a sincere heart, those who refuse to gossip, harm their neighbors or speak evil of their friends, those who despise sinners, honor faithful followers of the Lord and keep their promises and those who lend money without charging interest and who can't be bribed to lie about innocent people. That is a description of a noble person.

Doing the right thing is not always easy. Sometimes, it can place you in an uncomfortable position at work, with friends and families or at church. God desires us to be noble and upstanding. We are to follow His lead in whatever we do in life.

Amazing

How amazing are the deeds of the LORD! All who delight in him should ponder them. Psalm 111:2 NLT

He has done marvelous things, praise the Lord!

Every day, God's handiwork is amazing to see and hear. To hear the laughter of a toddler, or to see a rainbow in the sky after the rain falls, makes me smile. What other amazing things has God done in your life? The first thing that comes to mind is that we woke up and have activity in our limbs to get around. Next, we're able to breathe and our hearts are beating. Another thing is some have children, spouses or others we call family. All of this is amazing, because God has provided for us our needs and some of our wants. He didn't have to do it, but He did. As you look back on your life and you begin to think things over, surely you can say that you have a testimony of how amazing God has been in your life. As we come upon the Christmas season, I implore you to sing like the psalmist did in Psalm 96:7 (MSG) Bravo, God, Bravo! Everyone join in the great shout: Encore! In awe before the beauty, in awe before the might. God the Son coming in human flesh is simply beautiful, mighty and amazing.

December 20

Teachable

Come, my children, and listen to me, and I will teach you to fear the LORD. Psalm 34:11 NLT

Think back to when you were a small child, maybe three or four years old. It was summer time, and you wanted to put on your new sneakers. The only problem with wearing the new sneakers was you didn't know how to tie them. You were disappointed and frustrated. You sat in the middle of the floor and pouted. An adult came along and asked you what was wrong. And you began to tell him/her with all of the vocabulary that you could at that age. He/she looked at you and said, "I'll teach you." Immediately, your mood and attitude changed. The adult saw a teachable moment, and you were like a sponge, ready to be taught.

The smartest person in the world doesn't know everything and neither do we. The best teacher is the best student. No matter how old you are, remain teachable. Be teachable, whether at work, home, church or school. When you remain teachable, you have the tendency to teach and mentor others. Remember, each one, teach one, so both can grow together.

Honor

The payoff for meekness and fear of God is plenty and honor and a satisfying life. Proverbs 22:4 MSG

Reflect on how we, as a society, honor people from all walks of life. We give them flowers, erect a statue, give out awards, provide pay raises or promotions. We speak well of the wealthy so they can contribute to the famous people. However, as believers, we honor people because they are our brothers and sisters in Christ. This honor is because of God's love. We are created in God's image (Genesis 1:26-27). We are peculiar. We're not like a giraffe, goat or chicken. We make unique contributions to the body of Christ and our local church. Because you are unique and peculiar (1 Peter 2:9), you are special in God's sight. Just as you are special in God's sight, so are your fellow believers. Take time to honor them and let them know they are precious in God's sight, too. Remember, we're all created in the image of God. Be devoted to one another in love. Honor one another above yourselves (Romans 12:10 NIV).

Ambition

We pleaded with you, encouraged you, and urged you to live your lives in a way that God would consider worthy. For he called you to share in his Kingdom and glory. 1 Thessalonians 2:12 NLT

Goals, goals, goals. We hear everyone tell us we should have goals in our lives. Go get married.

Have a baby.

Go to school.

Go back to school.

Go higher in your job.

All of these are great goals. One would say that you were very ambitious to go for them all, if not most of them. How ambitious are you to have a better relationship with Christ and your fellow brothers and sisters? How ambitious are you to seek the will of God? As believers, our ultimate goal is to be with Him in heaven. Our daily ambition should be to commune with God morning, noon and night (Daniel 6:10, Mark 1:35, Psalm 5:2-3). Our daily ambition should be to seek His face (Psalm 105:4) and to hear from God (Psalm 4:1). Remember to, press on to reach the end of the race and receive the heavenly prize for which God, through Christ Jesus, is calling us (Philippians 3:14 NLT). There's a crown waiting for you.

Nourishment

About this time another large crowd had gathered, and the people ran out of food again. Jesus called his disciples and told them, "I feel sorry for these people. They have been here with me for three days, and they have nothing left to eat. If I send them home hungry, they will faint along the way. For some of them have come a long distance. Mark 8:1-3 NLT

God is not too busy to be concerned about your needs. There are times in our lives where we feel that God is not concerned about us or the things that we deserve. That simply is not true. God is aware of our wants and needs for our everyday lives. Remember in Matthew 6:31-32, Jesus says not to worry about having enough. God the father already knows. There is nothing too big for God to handle. Consider the child who needs nourishment. They need all of the essential vitamins in order to grow and be strong. As believers, we, too, need nourishment. We need nourishment from the Earth (food), and we need spiritual nourishment (Word of God) daily. In order to grow spiritually, we must feast on the Word of God regularly. In other words, we must commune with God through prayer, study and daily meditation. Don't forget to feed your soul daily, just like you feed your body daily.

December 24

Risk of Faith

Jesus said to her, "Daughter, you took a risk of faith, and now you're healed and whole. Live well, live blessed! Be healed of your plague." Mark 5:34 MSG

What kind of risks have you taken lately? Have you quit a job without having one in the wings? Ever get so angry that you cursed at your boss not knowing what the consequences would be? Have you applied for a job you didn't feel you were qualified to handle? We've all taken risks in life, some big and some small. In Mark 5:25-34, we find the woman with the issue of blood. She bled day in and day out for twelve long years. She was considered unclean and was isolated from her family and friends according to the Jewish law. She had taken all sorts of risks concerning her health. She went to every physician possible in order to get well. But all failed her. She heard about the miracles Jesus performed throughout the towns. She thought to herself, "All I have to do is get to Him. To touch His garment." She took a risk of faith to get to Jesus. She risked her life, her dignity and her pride just to get to Jesus. You, beloved, can take a risk of faith as well. Whether it's a new job, new career, new relationship or anything else you can think of, take a step of faith to go after your dreams. Big or small, take the risk with Jesus on your side.

December 25

Open-Hearted

But God showed his great love for us by sending Christ to die for us while we were still sinners. Romans 5:8 NLT

To be open-hearted means for one to express or display one's warm and kindly feelings without concealment. When I reflect on what Christ did on Calvary, I get overwhelmed. I think about how I've messed up over the years. I think about how I did God wrong and turned my back on Him. But because of His undying love for me, He still forgave me. His heart remained open, just waiting for me to stop acting like a spoiled brat. Who can't love God and His unmerited favor?

To be open-hearted also gives the appearance of having an open hand or open arms. Our hands and arms are open when we're ready to receive something or someone. As believers, we are to be like Christ in all that we do. One of the things we struggle with is to be open to forgiveness. We struggle with this, because we don't want to feel the pain of being hurt again. But just like Christ forgave those that betrayed Him, we also need to forgive those who did us wrong. Jesus was open to receive us as sinners. Let us be open-hearted to receive others.

December 26

Charity

Three things will last forever, faith, hope and love, and the
greatest of these is love. 1 Corinthians 13:13 NLT

Our faith lasts forever, because we place our faith in the everlasting Father. Our hope lasts forever because it is built on Jesus' blood and righteousness. Our love lasts forever because God is the Alpha and Omega. God is love, now and forever more.

1 Corinthians is often considered the "love chapter" of the Bible. Paul basically says if we do great things, such as, feed the homeless, take care of the sick and give to the poor, without love in our hearts, it's fruitless. In verses 4 through 7, he goes on to describe what love really is: patient, kind, not jealous and not rude. It is not selfish and doesn't keep a record of wrongdoings. It doesn't rejoice when bad things happen. Love doesn't give up. Love is hopeful, and it endures through every instance. And, at the end of the day, love lasts forever. Love is greater than everything else. As you go about your day today, remember to give the love of Jesus to all who crosses your path.

December 27

Hope

So be strong and courageous, all you who put your hope in the LORD! Psalm 31:24 NLT

Edward Mote wrote the hymn "My Hope is Built on Nothing Less." In this hymn, he speaks of God's grace. He tells of applying God's grace to one's life and finally, he speaks of how real God's grace is in the life of the believer. As believers in Jesus Christ, we don't live as the world does. Our faith and hope solely rely on Jesus Christ, our Solid Rock, our Creator. As Edward Mote says, all other ground is sinking sand. In other words, when you stand on Christ, He won't let you down. When you stand on Christ, you are lifted up with Him, because of Him. Don't get weary in well-doing. Things to remember about hope:

❖ It is based on God's faithfulness

❖ It comes from trusting Christ

❖ It comes from remembering and reflecting on all that God has done for us

❖ It grows as we continue to depend on God in difficult times

❖ It grows as we remember the promise of the Resurrection

Christ is our ultimate hope in the world.

December 28

Endurance

And endurance develops strength of character, and character strengthens our confident hope of salvation. Romans 5:4 NLT

I didn't play basketball until I got to college. I used to watch it on television and while I was in high school. But I really had no idea what it took to actually play the game. Training for the season started with running, followed by weight training and learning how to handle the ball. Initially, I was winded and out of breath. But as I kept practicing, my endurance and tolerance for the rigorous game grew.

In life, no matter where you come from, you will encounter hard times. As my grandmother would say, "Live a little, and you'll understand what I mean." Many times, in life, we are thrown curveballs, face mountains to climb and roadblocks to avoid. In all of our encounters, God is building our endurance. Endurance denotes building stamina. No one starts off running a marathon or triathlon without months of training beforehand. Over time, you're able to run longer, control your breathing and pick up the pace while you run. Romans 5:3-5 tells us that when we run into hard challenging times, it helps us to develop our endurance. This, in turn, builds our strength of character, and our character builds our hope of salvation, and our hope won't let us down because of the Holy Spirit that lives in us. If you ever get tired or weary, don't give up. Hold on tightly to God's hands. He will guide you along the way.

December 29

Love Fulfilled

For God loved the world so much that he gave his one and only Son, so that everyone who believes in him will not perish but have eternal life. John 3:16 NLT

Many of us have gone through life trying to find love. We look for it in our children and spouses. We look for it in the things that we buy: cars, purses, vacations, etc. But at the end of the day, we've discovered that our love wasn't fulfilled in things and other people. When God sent His son, Jesus, to earth, that was the ultimate love fulfilled. As we go through life, we must change our focus. We must cultivate our faith and belief in our relationship with our Savior, Jesus Christ. When we cultivate our relationship with Christ, we will experience God's forgiving love. When we cultivate our relationship, we know that God's love is beyond measure. When we cultivate our relationship, we will experience God's sacrificial love. When we cultivate that relationship, we will have our love fulfilled. Apostle John sums it up this way, We, though, are going to love—love and be loved. First we were loved, now we love. He loved us first (1 John 4:19 MSG). Go through your day reflecting on the love of Christ, just for you.

December 30

Leadership

Work hard and become a leader, be lazy and become a slave.
Proverbs 12:24 NLT

Point to yourself and say, "I am a leader."

What are some godly leadership principles? One would need to consider a few qualities of an effective leader. An effective leader perseveres through difficult times. He/she is able to delegate and appreciates the work of others. An effective leader recognizes his/her limitations and cultivates good character qualities.

Leadership has nothing to do with a title or a position. It is in your ability to lead and to follow, yet be an independent thinker. No matter where you are in life, you are a leader. Whether you are a certified nursing assistant, assistant director of nursing or a housekeeper, you are a leader. It doesn't matter if you're a pew warmer or the pastor, my friend, you are a leader. Go forward with God on your side. Stand in the God-given authority and be the leader God created you to be.

December 31

Enlarge

Seek the Kingdom of God above all else, and live righteously, and he will give you everything you need. Matthew 6:33 NLT

How many times in life did you ask God to increase your territory? In other words, you asked God to bless you more than what you already had. We want God to bless us with more and more; however, many times we are unprepared for what comes our way because our reasons for wanting more is not in alignment with God's will. Matthew tells us that we are to go and seek God before anything else. We are to live right in His eyes. And if we do that, He will give us what we need. We have a lot of wants in our lives. But God gives us what we need. There are many times that they are not the same. But God knows best. Trust in the Lord, with all your heart, and lean not to your own understanding. King Solomon tells us in Proverbs 3:5-6 (MSG) the following: Trust in the Lord with all your heart; do not depend on your own understanding. Seek his will in all you do, and he will show you which path to take. As our leading verse, Matthew 6:33 says, seek God first and God will give you what you need.

Biographies

Mrs. Chiketa Kelly-Dale, LPN

Mrs. Kelly-Dale is the owner of New Direction Home Healthcare of DFW Inc. In 2020 she launched 3 new businesses: CKD Hospice and Palliative Care Inc., ADF Homecare Services LLC & Be Scentsible by CKD LLC. Her passion is helping those in need. She strives daily to be a positive influence in the lives of all that she encounters. She is the mother to three young men, and played an active role in rearing two other young men. She is a proud grandmother of four amazing grand babies who affectionately call her Honey. She is the youngest child of Louis & Alice Kelly and the wife of Grady Dale. Her purpose in writing this devotional is to inspire those who inspire others daily.

To contact the author:
Website: CPR4thesoul.com

Rev. Dr. Jonanna Bryant, DNP

Dr. Jonanna Bryant is currently a nurse consultant for the Centers for Medicare and Medicaid Services. She received her doctor of nursing practice from Walden University. Her doctoral project is entitled Characteristics of an Informal Caregiver: An integrative review. Dr. Bryant is the founder/CEO of Nursing with Dr. J. Bryant and Professional Black Nurse Alliance. She is an international conference speaker and preacher. And she is currently an associate minister at Southern Baptist Church in Philadelphia, PA. Dr. Bryant's life scripture is Esther 4:14b "…for such a time as this." Dr. Bryant believes that her life is not her own and her life experiences are to help others along the way in life.

To contact the author:
FB: https://www.facebook.com/WalkByFaith
Email: DrJbryantRN@gmail.com
Website: WalkbyFaithdevotional.com

Dr. Bridgette Jenkins, DNP

Dr. Bridgette Jenkins is a woman of God, servant, Nurse, motivational speaker, educator, prayer warrior, autoimmune disease warrior, mother, grandmother, friend, mentor, and coach. She is called to serve the people of God and she does it with love and compassion. Dr. Jenkins is the owner of Health Education Institute where she teaches lifesaving courses to healthcare providers and the public. She also offers a variety of courses to healthcare providers to help them stay current on updates and changes within the healthcare arena. Dr. Jenkins is currently the radio and podcast host for Bounce Back Monday's with Dr. B. Dr. Jenkins is actively involved in her church and community. She is a mother to three adult children and a miniature schnauzer named Dallas. She is also MiMi to two adorable grandsons.

To contact the author:
Website: DrBridgette.com

Ms. Onissa Mitchell, MSN, RN, FNP

Onissa S. Mitchell is a Family Nurse Practitioner who believes in addressing the emotional and spiritual aspects of each patient to reverse physical illness bringing healing to the mind, body, and spirit. Her philosophy is to treat people as you want to be treated and find beauty in everything. Ms. Mitchell's positive attitude and confidence in the spirit of people has allowed her to be a light in the darkness of her patients and to those who have the privilege of knowing her. She is a proud member of St. Louis Baptist Church in Tyler, Texas. Ms. Mitchell is also an entrepreneur. She is a Certified CPR Instructor and the Owner/CEO of Healing Hearts CPR where she equips her clients with lifesaving knowledge and skills necessary to perform high-quality Basic Life Support, CPR, and First Aid. She is also a Certified Collector and Breathe-Alcohol Technician at her second company, East Texas Drug and DNA Testing. Ms. Mitchell uses her expertise to ensure her client's workplace remain drug and alcohol-free.

To contact the author:
FB: https://www.facebook.com/ChoZenFNP
IG: https://www.instagram.com/godschozenfnp
Email: chozenfnp@gmail.com
Website: chozenfnp.com

Dr. Michelle Spears, DNP

Dr. Michelle Spears is a Nurse Manager at the VA Medical Center in Philadelphia, PA. Dr. Spears is also a adjunct professor at the University of Phoenix. She has a passion for teaching and mentoring of students. She obtained her doctorate of nursing practice from Walden University. Dr. Spears has strong spiritual values and believes that God has called her to the area of nursing to not only care for patients but to have an impact on the quality of care nurses provide. Dr. Spears is a member of The Church of Christian Compassion in Philadelphia, Pa.

To contact the author:

Website: GiftOfAHealinghand.com